A Love Letter to Thomas
My Journey Through Grief

Eve Chauvel

What people are saying about
A Love Letter to Thomas:
My Journey Through Grief

"In *A Love Letter to Thomas*, Eve Chauvel points out that when a loved one passes suddenly, beyond the shock, sadness, and grieving, there lies the emptiness of a void that can never be filled — nor should it be. Eve is living testimony that, in the spaciousness of enough time, the best way to honor that relationship is to re-enter and mindfully engage in life, knowing that we are not less because of that loss, but more, because we carry the imprint of that person's essence in our expanded heart forever. If you have experienced a sudden loss, read *A Love Letter to Thomas*. It will give more meaning, purpose, and peace to your journey."
— Dennis Merritt Jones, DD - Award-winning author of *The Art of Uncertainty-*
How to Live In the Mystery of Life and Love It

"A story of love and grief, Eve Chauvel brings meaning to the unavoidable. Her book will bring you to tears and at the same time explain how faith gave her the strength to see herself as a blessing and not a victim. This book is a new narrative about the infinite nature of life."
— Rev. Dr. Jim Turrell,
author of *When It's Time to Leave*

"Your life can change in an instant. One day everything can seem grand and loving and then — the next moment — it can be turned completely upside down. This is a touching and true story about one woman's journey back

to peace and self-love, after experiencing the devastation of tragically and suddenly losing her husband. Through Eve's captivating writing, *A Love Letter to Thomas* shows us that our challenges can sometimes bring out our greatest strengths. This is a must read for everyone."
— Rev. Janet Moore, Assistant Minister/
Youth and Family Ministry

"Eve Chauvel is a source of inspiration. And *A Love Letter to Thomas* is a gifted read about the journey of true love, and an alternate way to empower anyone faced with loss and experiencing grief. Eve gives the reader deep insights, demonstrating that there is a way to heal through using Spiritual Mind principles as taught by Dr. Ernest Holmes."
— Rev. Carla Schiratis

"Eve's story is a remarkable one of love, laughter, loss, and a life gained through what may seem like inexplicable tragedy. This is a story of self-discovery and an understanding of the deepest aspects of connection. Everyone who has ever experienced unprecedented circumstances should read this book. Beautifully written, it is a story of transitions, new beginnings, great completions, and of the essence of what it means to be human. This is a gem of a read."
— Afrah Salahuddin, RScP.

"As I read *A Love Letter to Thomas*, I could hear Eve saying 'I choose Life.' And she chose it without qualifications. Whether on one of her cruises, or creating the Celebration of Life for Thomas... (it all) exemplifies her high regard for a life well-lived. This was an adventure I did not want to put down. It reminded me of my capacity for 'choosing Life,' only this time the life a Child of God could have, without fear, and open to all of life's experiences."
— Janet Foster, MS in Conflict Analysis (CAE)

"I felt like I was a witness to Eve's transformation through living her spiritual beliefs. Even before Thomas's death, she was already becoming a different person, and that's a very powerful message. I can't think of a better way to demonstrate the power of Science of Mind beliefs, than to show how it can get you through a horrible, traumatic loss of a loved one."
— Laura Morrison, PhD.

"Wow! Heart-wrenching, but descriptive and precise. The writing was so clear, you took me there with you. Thank you for sharing such intimate and personal details.... I am sorry you lost your husband. It reminds us how life is a gift and precious, every moment — especially with the ones we love and cherish the most. Blessings to you. May you be guided, loved, comforted."
— Julie Armenta Smith, Owner of Armenta Learning Academy, Laguna Niguel, CA

"Eve was correct: I needed tissues! Knowing the parties involved made reading Eve's words even more difficult. I am both moved by her ability to share the story on paper, as well the clarity of her vision of that experience. She is a masterful storyteller!"
    "Keep writing, my friend.
    The world needs your words."
— Mara Pennell

"It's like a beautiful puzzle-in-progress that got knocked to the floor - flying apart! - and the reader gets to accompany Eve as she mindfully, lovingly, puts it back together, only to discover a whole beautiful and new image emerging."
— Anne Perrah, Ph.D., RScP.

Dedication

To the dear, beloved Soul who gave the world
The *New* Gospel of Thomas:
"Be Nice"

To my daughter Kelsey,
the light in my life,
who has always shown me the way.
I love you, pumpkin.

Also, to the new love of my life,
Hugh Foster. You have shined a new
light on the world for me.

I love you, honey.

Foreword

A Love Letter to Thomas is a lovely stone in the cairn of Eve Chauvel's life experience thus far. She already had important life-changing experiences that opened her to self-exploration. My colleague and husband, Dr. Salvatore R. Maddi, and I have known her for over two decades, first as her teachers, mentors, and then as dear friends. She enrolled in our course on Stress Management: How to navigate stressful circumstances in times of change — what we call 'hardy coping.'

Eve embraced the learning fully, eager to learn how to turn adversity into new opportunities for learning, self-understanding, and betterment. She was then an undergraduate student at UCI, majoring in Psychology & Social Behavior in the School of Social Ecology, minoring in Management. Her young marriage to a controlling man, and raising a child on her own, were the spiritual impetus for twists, turns, and self-discoveries yet to come. Eve embraces both joy and grief as chances to awaken spiritually.

As you will find in the poignant story that is the impetus of this book, Eve Chauvel is not asleep in this life. I admire her resilience, courage, and inspired approach to her life. It is my honor to know her, to watch this vibrant, beautiful woman embrace joyful and heartbreaking changes fully. And, to watch her creatively use the difficulties presented to her as opportunities for spiritual growth, for herself and others.

Once my student, Eve Chauvel became my teacher. I know you will love her as I do, intimately sharing her journey through incredible grief. You are invited to go with her as she travels the path of vibrant life, continuing to live it fully.

— Dr. Deborah Khoshaba-Maddi
Clinical and Health Psychologist
President of the Hardiness Institute and Founder of the blog Psychology in Everyday Life.

Preface

      This is a personal memoir that covers the seven-year relationship with my late husband, Thomas. Three years of long-distance romance led to four years of marital bliss. My intention for this story is to illustrate how my undying commitment to the Science of Mind philosophy allowed me to move through the darkest days of my life with faith, hope, and grace. Read on....

Table of Contents

*"It is only with the heart that one can see rightly.
What is essential is invisible to the eye."*
— Antoine De Saint-Exupéry

*"Il n'y a qu'avec le coeur qu'on peut voir juste.
L'essentiel est invisible pour les yeux."*

Prologue

Thomas never enjoyed novels, save one: *The Little Prince.* Soft-covered and dog-eared, it was always with him. French was his native tongue, yet this version was in English. He never told me how he had acquired it.

A man of few possessions, Thomas nestled this novel in his rugged, burlap men's satchel, guaranteeing its safe passage as he traversed all seven continents. Over the course of his mere 43 years on the planet, Thomas created a lifestyle that enabled him to live, work, and travel at will. Standing six-foot-two, slim and fit, there was a gentleness about him. Anyone who was fortunate enough to be in his presence knew they had been touched by an angel. His hazel-brown eyes sparkled, displaying a curiosity about life, people, and radiating genuine kindness. Never quick to anger, he had a calm demeanor that quickly put people at ease. It's no wonder I was attracted to him.

My heart was aching for a soul-filled type of love that my current marriage of 11 years was lacking. I knew I had suppressed my desire for a more adventurous life for far too long. Little did I know the moment I first saw him, Thomas would lead me to the greatest adventure of all: a realization of unconditional love and forgiveness.

---

*"Character is the willingness to accept responsibility
for one's own life. It is the source
from which self-respect springs."*
— Joan Didion

Paradise Found

A trip to French Polynesia — I was going to paradise! Seven days on an all-inclusive cruise ship named Paul Gauguin. Would my two years of high school French suffice on board to interact with the crew? Only time would tell. For me, having grown up in Southern California conditioned me to become a worshiper of the Sun and my excitement was palpable. My current husband was less enthused. He did not enjoy bathing, in either Sun or sea. Additionally, he admitted to not knowing how to swim. So the thought of being on a cruise ship in the middle of an ocean provoked a great deal of internal anxiety. Despite his trepidation, he agreed to escort me on one of the last travel experiences we would share together.

———————

The primary activity of the first day on board entailed a safety drill.

"I will be calling off your last name and suite number," announced the young man with a heavy French accent, dressed in a perfectly pressed white uniform. He looked to be in his early 30's.

My heart skipped a beat. Tingles ran up and down my spine. The sensation was delicious. My inner voice whispered, *I wonder what his hugs feel like* — followed immediately by my shock at having entertained that thought.

An attractive woman with mid-length silver hair stood to my right. She nudged me with her elbow, turning her mouth towards my ear.

"I feel that too. I've been on this ship before and tried to make contact with him."

"Really?" I questioned.

"Indeed. No luck. Either he's taken, gay, or a strict rule-follower. Fraternizing with guests is highly discouraged. All I can say is get in line, honey."

The activity concluded and we returned to our suite to unpack and get ready for dinner.

"Just my luck! I started my period," I told my husband.

"Well, you know what that means. I wonder if there are any sharks around. How will you stay safe snorkeling? They can smell blood, you know," my husband retorted.

I thought, *Who cares?* He's not going to drown my enthusiasm. I won't let anything stop me from enjoying submerging myself in these crystalline waters.

Each passing day, my thoughts continued to turn towards the events which led me to this point in my life, particularly that of committed relationships. My first marriage of six years ended in divorce and my current marriage was hanging by threads. Was our twenty-year age difference finally showing its true colors? Congestion in my throat was continual. My voice was yearning to be heard. A cry for help seemed lackluster. My emotional prison guards could no longer hold me. A full break-out was imminent.

Each day seemed to bring with it the promise of crossing paths with Thomas. Not only did he work as the Maître 'd Hotel in the ship's restaurant, but he was also the wine steward, commonly referred to as Sommelier. Perfect. I had been deepening my understanding about wine since completing a vacation home build in Napa Valley. I anticipated trying out my knowledge in a new environment and perhaps even testing out my rusty French.

"I typically start with Champagne, yet I'm curious about this Sauvignon Blanc. It's from New Zealand and I've never been there," I offered at dinner.

Thomas lifted the bottle gently and pointed to the label. "This is a 2009 Picton Bay from Marlborough, on New Zealand's South Island. It's very fragrant on the nose, fresh, vibrant, and crisp like a Granny Smith apple. The perfect aperitif." I sensed that I had seen this wine previously, yet I couldn't recall exactly where. Again, my soul was overcome with a deep understanding that he and I were connecting. I struggled to dismiss this feeling. After all, as a small voice gently reminded me, I was still a married woman.

One evening, several nights into the trip, I found myself out walking, alone, on the upper deck. Feeling the warm breeze that lovely moonlit night, my thoughts turned inward. On a night like this, I didn't want to feel so alone, so melancholy. What I wanted was a deep sense of connection, some of the fire that I had desired for so long now. What I felt instead was the weight of honest questioning: Did I feel safe? Free? Supported to be my authentic self in this marriage?

The questions kept coming.

Was I even cut out for marriage? In previous generations, marital promises were made in a time when life expectancy was much shorter. How long would my life span be? Was I truly getting what my heart wanted from this relationship? Does the promise I made continue to support my self-worth?

By all accounts, my life was amazing. I traversed between two gorgeous California homes, a beach house in Corona del Mar and a farmhouse nestled within a vineyard in Napa Valley. Working as an independent consultant for non-profit organizations gave me purpose. Having control over my schedule afforded me flexibility which was empowering. From an outsider's perspective, there was nothing missing. Still, I couldn't shake the feeling of wanting more.

A Love Letter to Thomas

"The person I am seeking is also seeking me.
We are being brought together on the checkerboard of life."
— Louise L. Hay

The Early Years

Over the course of the next year, Thomas and I communicated on a regular basis through the various means available, predominantly Facebook Messenger and Skype. The only direct contact we had happened onboard the Paul Gauguin while taking a photo in the restaurant during the last night on board. Dreams about him were sporadic. Yet one spring morning I awoke, startled by a vision of Thomas wearing a white uniform, dripping wet. There was nothing in the dream to indicate the cause of his condition. This puzzled me.

Later that same morning, he called. An unusual event as he was currently working a nine-month contract with Regent Seven Seas circumnavigating South America, employed as the Head Sommelier.

"Bonjour, Eve", he said with that sultry French accent of his.

"Bonjour, Thomas. To what do I owe the pleasure?"

"I have bad news: I am in quarantine."

"Oh no!" I exclaimed "What happened? How are you?"

"I have come down with a fever and am sweating profusely."

My fingers lost their grip on the phone momentarily. A jolt of energy traveled rapidly from my head to my toes. I was speechless. Thomas was dripping wet — just like in my dream! The coincidence was incomprehensible, yet I know that there is no such thing in the mind of Spirit.

This demonstrated our spiritual, soul-filled connection for me, while giving me unmistakable clarity that pursuing this relationship was my right path.

I craved time alone. My inner child was screaming for solace. I was desperate for a personal retreat that would afford me time to reflect. With my mother's 71st birthday approaching, I felt time together would be beneficial for us both, particularly since she had recently separated from her husband. She lives in Port Angeles WA, located on the Olympic Peninsula, directly across from Vancouver Island, British Columbia, with the Strait of Juan de Fuca separating both land masses. After visiting my mother, the trip would entail solo travel to Victoria for five days. I booked a small cabin to stay in, rented a car, and booked the ferry passage. This would be my inaugural solo trip without friends or family accompanying me. It felt freeing and long overdue to plan a trip just for me.

During our visit, my mom introduced me to the Center for Spiritual Living (CSL) in Sequim. I had never heard of this organization before and was excited to learn more about this philosophy and way of life. I quickly learned there was a magical aspect to this belief system. Not a traditional organized religion, but rather a system based on science and open at the top — warm, loving, and accepting of all without judgment or condemnations. The experience was incredibly uplifting, and I thought to myself that there must surely be a similar place in Orange County. I made a mental note to research CSL when I returned home.

With a bit of trepidation, I took the ferry over to Victoria on July 23rd. Spirit guided me on my journey and for five days, I nurtured my soul. Each day was a new adventure. Having the freedom to choose when and where

I wanted to go was liberating. Being immersed in nature gave me an opportunity to truly connect with Source. Needless to say, when my time was over, I realized big changes were in the works. Upon returning to Orange County, I knew I had to make a shift in my spiritual life. I looked up Centers for Spiritual Living and found there was a location holding services at the University Synagogue in Irvine. Years ago, an ice rink called The Big Red Barn occupied that location. I recalled the structure with fond memories, as one of my daughter Kelsey's birthday parties was celebrated there.

Arriving on a Sunday morning for services, I felt unconditional love the moment I walked through the door. It was as if I were receiving a warm virtual hug. I was home.

To my surprise, I recognized someone! The Senior Minister's daughter, Erica Turrell, had been one of my daughter's middle school teachers. She recently began teaching at the school, being very gifted at instructing the students in their vocal capabilities.

My experience at the spiritual center was extremely fulfilling, and I returned week after week. My husband came with me for a while, yet I knew we were on different paths. Dr. Jim Turrell had recently written a book called *How to Spiritually Complete a Relationship*, available in PDF format. That book was just the impetus for me to realize I needed a change. I told my husband that I wanted more solo trips. He was noticeably displeased, but didn't question my desire.

Thomas and I continued to communicate and coincidentally, he was ending a contract in Europe, visiting the same countries where my husband and our friends were traveling. The trip began on land in Italy in

Florence, Lake Como, and Venice, then it continued on sea aboard a Seabourn cruise ship embarking out of Venice and sailing to Italy, Croatia, and Greece. At this point in our relationship, my husband and I were traveling more as friends than partners, due to waning affections. My thoughts continued to imagine a life with Thomas, despite him being eight years my junior.

That winter, Thomas took a contract with a cruise company called Ponant, the only company that was French-based. His first contract began with — of all things — a two-month trek in Antarctica! After which, he would cross the Atlantic Ocean and head for the Mediterranean.

My husband and I eased into the conversation about how we would dissolve our relationship. A trial separation was agreed upon. He moved to our second home in Napa Valley and I remained in Corona Del Mar. I dove deep into my spiritual growth by attending a class taught by Reverend Janet Moore and Reverend Carla Schiratis. It was based on the insightful book *This Thing Called You* by Ernest Holmes, and it gave me agency to take a leap of faith, requesting a formal separation from my husband.

In February of 2013, I traveled to our home in Napa Valley for a short weekend to entertain a nephew and his girlfriend who were visiting from Oklahoma. During that time, I collected all my belongings and said goodbye to the house that my husband and I had built together. It was bittersweet. However, I knew in my heart of hearts that it was the right thing to do for my growth and expansion. Kelsey, 19 at the time, picked me up at the airport and stayed in Corona Del Mar. After unpacking I asked Kelsey to join me in my room.

"Pumpkin, I have something to tell you."

A Love Letter to Thomas

Kelsey stared at me; a concerned expression written on her face. My hand reached for hers.

"Your step-father and I are getting a divorce."

"No, no, no, no!"

"Yes, sweetheart. I need to move on from this relationship."

"I knew it! I knew something was wrong. You never travel with your big suitcase."

She had seen the evidence that the marriage was crumbling. An old soul, Kelsey seemed to be dialed into intimate knowledge about spiritual truths, elements of nature, and people's emotions. These traits would serve her well in the years to come.

My heart felt her pain. Another broken family chapter in her story. Her dad had recently remarried for the fourth time. Now, I was ending my second marriage. The branches in her family tree seemed to be breaking off in double armloads, shattering her desire for any sense of familial normality. Yet, what is normal? For me, family is where you can feel accepted and embraced for who you are exactly as you show up. No judgment. No condemnation. No criticism. Fortunately for me, my newly-found spiritual family at O.C. Spiritual Center, formerly known as Center For Spiritual Living Newport-Mesa, provided me with that level of safety, belonging, and comfort.

To aid in my healing journey, I embraced various life preservers in the forms of meditation, reading, and walks on the beach. During one of my early morning meditations, sitting on lifeguard tower number five at

Corona del Mar State Beach, I distinctly heard Spirit speaking these words to me:

I am confident, I am strong,
I can cope with whatever comes along...

This drum-like beat was perfectly aligned with my state of consciousness. I continued to chant it while walking on the beach, feeling the sand beneath my bare feet, and the chilly sea water flowing over them, as gentle waves washed along the shore.

Not too long after I had officially taken solo occupancy of the home in Corona del Mar, my husband arrived to clear out his personal belongings. I gave him space to do so alone, without my presence. We agreed to have one last dinner together at the Side Door, an English-style pub in Corona del Mar. Sitting across from each other, we reflected on all the good that had been experienced during our courtship and marriage. The overarching tone was gratitude. Reaching across the table, we took each other's hands.

"It is a bit sad though," I said.

"Yes it is," was his reply.

The following day, I discovered a box tied with a ribbon. Stuck to the top was a post-it note with "13 Years" written on it. I opened the box, and found all the cards that I had given him for various holidays, birthdays, anniversaries, etc. I thought to myself, *what am I going to do with this?* Throwing them away felt awkward; shredding them seemed too aggressive. I decided to take them down to the fire pits at Corona Del Mar State Beach and have a love offering. We had experienced a tremendous amount of love and appreciation during our years together, yet it was time to release that into the Universe. The energy had to go somewhere, didn't it?

A few weeks later I learned that my husband was seriously dating a woman we had been acquainted with in Saint Helena. She managed the fitness center where we were members and also worked at a women's clothing boutique in town. We socialized with her periodically, including having her over for lunch at our home. I had sensed that she was attracted to my husband, so it came as no surprise to find out they were dating. Eventually, they married. My heart was happy to see that he had found love again.

In the spring of 2013, I decided to travel to France and then Spain for 10 days to meet up with Thomas while he had a short break between contracts. We met at the Marseille airport, where he picked up a rental car. We stayed at a hotel for two nights and then went on a road trip touring Province, the coastline of southwest France, and eventually Barcelona. It was a wild adventure filled with lovely scenery, wine, and good food. Coincidentally, before the trip I had purchased an iPad and met a lady named Julia who had traveled solo extensively and shared her experiences with me. I took some of her recommendations. It felt liberating to be on my own and traveling light. I had taken a class at Rooten's Luggage on how to pack efficiently with only carry-on luggage. I was astounded at what I learned!

My next solo trip was in August of 2013 on a ship where Thomas was working. My plan was for two weeks starting in Athens traveling to the Turquoise Coast of Turkey, back to Greece, then Croatia and Italy, ending in Venice.

The first week's theme was *Mama Mia*, with a

French-based theater company performing every night on board. I celebrated my birthday on board, wearing a white dress I had purchased at Bloomingdale's in Newport Beach's Fashion Island shopping mall. It was very simple, form fitting. I looked and felt fantastic! Little did I know, it would be the dress I would wear at our wedding a few years down the road.

Halfway through the second week, I was having so much fun, and with Thomas' birthday around the corner, August 14th, I decided to tack on a third week. It was one of the most spontaneous decisions I had ever made in my life! I contacted my travel agent, and she miraculously changed my flights and adjusted my schedule. I couldn't believe it! Another week of cruising and more time with Thomas. Even though it was 'disallowed,' he stayed in my stateroom with me. We connected on many different levels — I knew that we had a future together. Saying goodbye became more difficult with each parting. The emotions brought up unresolved grief in the form of separation anxiety. My newfound spiritual belief system became an integral part of my healing journey, allowing me to gain a deeper understanding of the root causes for these emotions.

Our long-distance relationship continued, as we embraced the ability to use technology for staying in touch and seeing each other whenever our schedules allowed. My first visit to Brittany was in February 2014, on Valentine's Day. It was cold and drizzly, very similar to Ireland. I brought Thomas a gift; a set of four homemade coasters made with corks from wine bottles. On the back I inscribed the words "Made with love... (Fait avec amour...) by Eve."

We enjoyed a lovely Valentine's Day meal in the restaurant at the local Manoir des Portes, a hotel and restaurant that Thomas' grandparents owned, and his parents operated when he was a child. Thomas' grandfather, Michel, was the primary landowner in this village and had sold off plots to buy this 16th century manor in 1959. The majestic building has a stone façade with pervasive character, bordered by a pond, and nestled within the heart of a superb park. It was situated near a lake, with gorgeous views of the village's small chapel and a handful of homes that could be seen from the hotel's entry gate. An old well resided in the middle of a grassy area.

Nearby, the ancient bread oven stood like a grandiose anchor in the corner of the property. This was the gathering spot from years ago, a community oven where villagers would take their formed loaves, or boules, to cook for the day. An annual "la fete du pain" took place here in early May. This is an annual festival of bread taking place from May eighth to the seventeenth where villagers celebrate the long-standing art of traditional French bread baking. What a delightful custom!

Our long-distance romance was moving along swimmingly. In June 2014, I launched into travel mode again. This time embarking on two back-to-back cruises with Ponant aboard the L'Austral. First leg was in the Baltic Sea followed by another in the Norwegian Fjords. In sum, I was on the ship for seventeen magical days.

The ports were lovely, so marvelous. I was continually pinching myself, hardly believing I was in these locations as a solo traveler! Yes, Thomas was with me some of the time, yet his breaks were quite short. Regardless, we took every opportunity to tour the cities together, enjoy a meal, and have a beer or glass of wine.

It was on this trip that we professed our undying

Eve Chauvel

love for each other, expressing a desire to spend the rest of our lives together regardless of where our home base was. What do you do when, something that seemed too good to be true, actually comes true?

A Love Letter to Thomas

"We live in an Eternal Presence of Pure Spirit whose
whole purpose is Good, whose whole desire is
constructive, and whose whole feeling toward
us is one of Love and Compassion."
— Ernest Holmes

California Dreaming

The first time Thomas came to visit me in California was in the fall of 2014. A colleague of his, Sam Geffroy who he attended hospitality school with in France, lived in San Diego, approximately one hour away from my house. We went down and surprised him during lunch. Excitement filled the air as I observed them connecting and speaking in their charming native tongue. The two reconnected and spoke often. Sam was aware of a French cafe opening in Newport Beach, in the former space occupied by Pascal.

Thomas met the owner, Laurent Vrignaud, and they quickly agreed to have him work the lunch shift and an occasional evening dinner. Thomas thrived, finding his niche and connecting with other French-born individuals living in the area. He was feeling out what it was like to exist in a new environment; on land and with more stability. We both had options and flexibility in terms of where we could live. We had declared our desire for a more permanent relationship. The larger question was where would we land? He hinted at working on a private yacht or in a luxury hotel anywhere in Southeast Asia. I was open and receptive. The world was our oyster and nothing would hold us back. The possibilities were endless!

And, the sea was calling Thomas. In early 2015, he signed up for a short-term contract with Ponant, meaning he would leave California and we would not see each other again for at least four months. My heart ached at the prospect.

That summer, I decided to leave the U.S. and travel with Thomas in Europe for three months. This act alone was stretching me, yet I continued to trust Spirit to guide me along the way. We spent one month in Rome — very exciting! At the end of our time in Rome together Thomas returned to work on a cruise ship for a short contract.

I was in Paris by myself for 10 days. I found it quite exhilarating; visiting places that Thomas had no desire to go to. We had rented a small apartment in the Saint-Germain-des-Prés area, and I took to visiting bookstores, dining alone, and exploring the city. It was easy for me to acclimate with my limited French, and I picked up on cues from the locals on how to somewhat disguise myself from the all-too-obvious tourist persona.

Despite the newfound freedom I was experiencing, my longing for companionship tugged at my soul. I reached out to Mara Pennell who helped me gain a deeper understanding of my soul's inner workings. After our lengthy discussion, she gave me a mantra to use whenever my heart needed comfort:

"Day by day I'm getting stronger and stronger and more self-sufficient. I can easily and happily wait for Thomas and the physical affection I get from him. My well-being comes from within me more and more, steadier, and more balanced every day."

I received a message from Thomas. He had decided this would be his last contract aboard a ship. He wanted to move to California and live with me. I was elated! The moment for us to move forward with the rest of our lives together was happening! My gratitude was overflowing, eager to see this plan come to fruition.

We began researching what type of visa would be appropriate for him to get, and how to navigate the system. We decided that a fiancé visa was out of the question because it would take too long to process and Thomas would need to stay in France until it was approved, which could be months. That was not what we wanted more of. We were ready to spend our lives together as soon as possible. Receiving advice from an immigration attorney referred by a friend, we decided a "tourist" visa was the best route and *then* we would "decide" to get married.

Throughout our courtship, I continually felt that our late grandparents, my grandmother Pauline (everyone called her Polly) and his grandparents Michel and Henriette, had been working behind the scenes to forge our life together as a married couple. To honor that intuition, we set a date of February 5, 2016, to get married. This date would have been my paternal grandmother's 100th birthday.

Our wedding was very simple. Our only guest was my daughter Kelsey, in addition to photographer Chuck Jensen and his wife Gail. Reverend Janet Moore officiated. It was a lovely scene, on the sand in Pirate's Cove, a short distance from our home in Corona Del Mar. We knew we were taking a chance having a wedding on the beach in February. As it turned out, it was the warmest on record!

I recall Thomas being very nervous. Perhaps he was reflecting on the fact that after his first marriage ended, he swore he would never get married again. Yet here we were, embarking on a lifelong journey together. Everything fell into place. I wore the white dress purchased for the *Mama Mia*-themed cruise, Thomas donned a gray blue suit, and Kelsey was dazzling in a vintage yellow dress. It was a beautiful ceremony. In Thomas' vows, he promised to bring me coffee in bed every morning. We filled a vessel of sand together, each selecting our favorite colors: yellow for me and blue for Thomas. We popped a bottle of champagne, and the six of us enjoyed it as the sun went down on our wedding day, February 5, 2016.

It was the happiest day of my life, aside from when Kelsey was born. Our previous marriages were now behind us both. I had finally arrived at the place where I was comfortable in my skin, being true to who I am, and feeling stronger than ever before in my spiritual journey as a human on this planet. An excerpt from my journal illustrates my emotions at that time:

"Just over 24 hours until Thomas and I get married! What a journey we have been on over the last three years. I am incredibly grateful for the path behind and ahead of me. Our life will be filled with love, patience, trust, and adventure. My deeply rooted faith in spiritual practices continues to grow. The evolution of my understanding of how the Science of Mind principles operate, aid, and support my ability to appreciate life in a more meaningful way.

So how do I feel about entering marriage again? The commitment now is such a different thing from prior times. My personal maturity and growing faith have a great deal to do with it. At the same time, being so connected to Thomas and having freedom to express myself in a safe space makes my experience better! I'm very blessed."

A Love Letter to Thomas

"The only bird that doesn't get a worm
is the bird that doesn't go out to get one."
— Mike Dooley

Professional Travelers

Thomas worked full-time at Moulin, and we applied for his temporary green card. Having a desire to do something else that would fulfill him, he started seeking other opportunities. The annual travel and adventure show was coming to Los Angeles, and we planned to attend. While walking around the convention space, we discovered a booth called Cruise Planners. Their theme color is green and there was no holding back in their expression of that. The sales staff greeted us, and Thomas struck up a conversation with one of the gentlemen.

We learned that Cruise Planners was a franchisor — and one of the leaders in the industry. Their partnership with American Express was attractive, because that validated the high level of service and quality they would provide to clients. Because of Thomas' history working on cruise ships, it seemed like a perfect fit for him.

I was still in a state of limbo, staying open and receptive to whatever the universe was bringing my way. During the conversation, Thomas learned that anyone who had previously been in the industry would receive a significant discount for buying into the business. That was quite attractive! Even though Thomas had spent most of his savings buying a house for his parents in Brittany, he had some funds left over, and he strongly desired a franchise.

In the following days, Thomas did his due diligence. He researched other franchise opportunities, spoke with existing Cruise Planners franchise owners, and finally decided to take a leap of faith buying into the business. I could tell there was fire in his belly, and excitement about maintaining his role in the travel industry, with his desire to be of service leading him down that path. There were two requirements: online training modules and in-person training to occur in Fort Lauderdale FL. He asked me if I would like to join him in the training — and in the business — and of course I said yes!

I began creating the foundational elements of running the business, establishing an LLC, opening a bank account, and getting the administrative side established. We didn't know what to name the business. After what seemed like hours of brainstorming, we decided on Seaview Voyage, mainly because we lived on Seaview Avenue. To our surprise, the domain name was available! Our motto: "To travel is to live!"

Our business grew rapidly, which I attributed to the connections Thomas made with customers at Moulin and my established circle of friends. We also took advantage of every opportunity to conduct 'research and development,' paying highly reduced travel agent rates to travel. One of our first experiences was a cruise to Alaska. Thomas had been there before while working, yet we wanted to experience it as passengers.

Month after month the business grew, and we enjoyed serving our clients. The focus was never on making money. We simply wanted to be the vehicle for people to create experiences with their loved ones and check destinations off their bucket lists.

We worked well together as a team and complemented each other's skillsets to a very high degree. I must admit there were times that I didn't agree with Thomas' approach to cultivating clients or responding to their needs. However, I always encouraged him to be his own unique self. We recouped his initial investment in the business within the first year and were on a very strong trajectory of growth. When we attended the Cruise Planners annual conferences, we were delighted to make connections with industry leaders and continue learning about new ships, unique destinations, and special benefits we could offer our clients.

Simultaneously, I continued my studies of the Science of Mind Philosophy, embarking on the two-year spiritual journey of becoming a Licensed Prayer Practitioner.

What is a Prayer Practitioner? The governing body, Centers for Spiritual Living, defines this role as a person of high spiritual consciousness and deep understanding of the spiritual nature of Life, where a deep and personal relationship with the Divine is prominent. The Licensed Spiritual Practitioner is trained in the study of The Science of Mind, and in the art, science and skill of Spiritual Mind Treatment, also known as Affirmative Prayer. Licensed Spiritual Practitioners are dedicated to the cause of helping others and offering sacred service. Licensed to practice professionally, practitioners are bound by a high code of ethics, while providing a safe and confidential space for clients.

I was committing myself to a serious undertaking, requiring weekly attendance at an evening class. I was grateful for Thomas' support and his generosity in co-creating a life where we both could thrive. Living and working together can pose challenges, yet we were able to navigate them with grace and ease. There was a tremendous amount of deep love and authentic respect between us. I felt like the luckiest woman on the planet.

It was not all work for Thomas and me. I practiced yoga at Yoga Works in Newport Beach three times a week, enjoyed meals with friends, and went dancing as often as my schedule allowed. Dancing is one of my favorite pastimes.

Thomas had been an avid soccer player most of his life, and he wanted to find a group of individuals he could bond with. One day, while out on a run, he came upon a group of young men playing soccer. They needed one more comrade. To their amazement, he was wearing the same color shirt that the team was wearing. To hear the other players tell it, they described Thomas as exceptional, almost professional. That day launched him into a thrice-weekly noontime game and lasting friendships. Two times, he even participated in tournaments where they won first place. Most of the players worked at Pacific Life. This was another coincidence, as my mother had worked there in the 1980s when it was known as Pacific Mutual Life Insurance.

A Love Letter to Thomas

> *"The stars are like letters that inscribe themselves*
> *at every moment in the sky.*
> *Everything in the world is full of signs.*
> *All events are coordinated.*
> *All things depend on each other.*
> *Everything breathes together."*
> *— Plotinus*

Au Revoir, Maman

Thomas was not a regular giver of tangible gifts, let alone jewelry. During our courtship, I suggested we take Gary Chapman's Love Languages quiz. Thomas agreed. We undertook this activity while sunbathing on the expansive French beach in Pléneuf-Val-André. This is a quiz to discover an individual's personal love language, what it means, and how a person can use it to better connect with loved ones. Results revealed Thomas' top two love languages were acts of service and quality time. Mine are physical touch and quality time. That said, anytime I received a token of his love, such as a bouquet of flowers or something edible, my heart welled-up with gratitude and appreciation.

I became accustomed to his style due to the numerous acts of service he demonstrated daily. Things such as bringing me coffee in bed each morning (which he had promised to do in his wedding vows), cooking me dinner every night (most mornings asking what I wanted to eat, then promptly finding a recipe to fulfill that desire), taking care to give me physical pleasure when an erotic moment arose, and often expressing his appreciation for me. So, when any significant holiday appeared on the calendar, I never expected anything above and beyond what had been my experience previously. Yes, I dropped hints that I desired an opal of some type, never having owned one of those treasures of our beautiful planet. After hearing Thomas' stories of visiting the opal mines in Australia, I was even more enamored of wearing such an extraordinary gem. Little did I know...

In the early morning of Saturday, July 21, 2018, Thomas received a call from his brother, Christophe, in

Wales. Their mother, Michele, and her husband Bernard, both 70 years old, had simultaneously been in a French hospital for close to two weeks, due to various medical conditions. They had recently relocated to the Brittany region of France after retiring in Senegal. Bernard awaited discharge while Michele was undergoing an additional MRI. During the procedure, she experienced a seizure and lapsed into a coma. The prognosis was dire: She might not survive the night. Thomas rushed into action, quickly booking a one-way flight from Los Angeles to Paris while packing a suitcase with items for an undetermined length of stay. Within 90 minutes we were on the road to Los Angeles International Airport.

His connecting flight through Canada was canceled, yet Thomas was offered an option to fly to London then on to Paris. Knowing that the window to see his mom was slowly shrinking, he took this option. After the train ride from Paris to Rennes, then Rennes to Lamballe, he was shuttled by an uncle directly to the hospital for a visit, late on July 22nd. Michele was barely hanging on.

Meanwhile, I booked a one-way ticket, departing the following day, Monday, July 23rd for an undetermined amount of time. My body shivered as I realized the significance of this date - it was the anniversary of our formal engagement.

As usual, I attended Sunday morning service, sharing with my spiritual community an update of what was unfolding, and I asked for prayer.

As I was checking in for my flight at LAX the following morning, Thomas called to say his mom had passed away. My heart sank. Attempting to control my emotions, I spent time in prayer and reflection. I fought to hold back public tears. My journey to France was filled with sadness, heaviness, and deep concern for Thomas. However, I was grateful that he had been able to see Michele before she died.

It took me a full 24 hours to get to Brittany via plane and train. Thomas greeted me at the station in Lamballe and we collapsed into each other's arms, embracing tightly. The French are not known to hug during times of sorrow. (This was something I would come to understand on a deeper level a few years later.) Despite this French penchant against public tears, I couldn't hold anything back. It was a tough time for the family as, according to Thomas, Bernard was not well-liked by his family in-law, the LeDrogoffs. He had not treated Michele with dignity or respect. He was continually emotionally and psychologically abusive. Thomas couldn't understand why she had to die and not Bernard — the one who abused his body with alcohol, a poor diet, and no exercise. To say his demeanor was cruel is an understatement.

Regardless, I was at Thomas' side throughout the arrangements for Michele's funeral, cremation, and succession (the French term for inheritance), as well as discussions surrounding Bernard's future care. I was willing to do whatever it took to help the family navigate this difficult moment. Of course, not knowing French limited my ability to participate fully. There were copious tasks to complete and schedules to coordinate. I desperately wanted to be of service. Trusting that Spirit would show me how, I surrendered to the experience.

The body was available for viewing and was placed in the "Hummingbird Room." Thomas was astonished by this. To his recollection, there are no hummingbirds in all of France. Additionally, he told me that there was a solitary dragonfly buzzing around outside the window, attempting to enter this space. I reflected on my time in

Bhutan where there were fields of dragon flies. Mother Nature was showing off again!

Thomas' father, Bernard, was there, exhibiting his curmudgeonly demeanor, as repellant as ever. I chose to sit with him and hold his hand. He was overcome with grief: tearful and distraught. I'm confident he felt abandoned, and perhaps a touch guilty. Michele had acted like a servant for him, tolerating his alcoholism and abusive tendencies. As Thomas saw it, she'd had enough of his behavior and was ready to leave the planet. I felt sorry for him.

"Why does he get to stay?" Thomas growled in an angry tone.

It was unfortunate that such a kindhearted, lovely lady would complete her time on this planet while the idiot (to use Thomas' words) got to stick around. His anger was evident.

"My love, if anything happened to me and you inherited the house in La Poterie, would you kick my dad out?" A concerned look crossed over Thomas' face.

"Of course not! Don't be silly. I would never do that to an infirm person, regardless of their state of mind and body. Don't you worry, my love."

Even Bernard's constant state of grumbling would not cause me to act so un-compassionately.

We stayed with Uncle Serge, one of Michele's three brothers, and his wife Jocelyn for one week, then we decided that our own accommodations were necessary for the remainder of our visit.

A Love Letter to Thomas

It was high summer season, and we were fortunate to find the last available apartment directly facing the boardwalk along the beach in Pléneuf Val Andre. Considering it was summer and demand was high, I was grateful we found a place; two bedrooms, a spacious kitchen, gorgeous views, a balcony overlooking a garden of hydrangeas, and at the last minute. It was a perfect respite from the tasks at hand. Breathing room for grief.

More tasks lay ahead of us, mostly pertaining to Bernard's in-home care and researching assisted living facilities. His health was poor. Decades of alcohol consumption coupled with a diet heavily laden in meat had caught up with him. Prostate cancer and other health ailments exacerbated his disdain for life and anything pleasant. No wonder Thomas was frustrated with picking up the pieces in the wake of his mother's death.

The most unusual task we undertook was to send thank you notes to everyone who sent a card of condolence or a flower arrangement. The reasons for this were not communicated to me. However, I came to understand that this is one of the rules of proper etiquette according to Emily Post, an American author and socialite. There was a time pressure to get these mailed, which for me, seemed to be such a burden for those grieving. I took on the responsibility once given the proper supplies, addresses, and script written in French. Grateful to be of service, I went to task and even enjoyed the process. Sometimes the easiest prayer you can ever say is a simple thank you.

As it turned out, we were able to complete our time in France by August seventh, my birthday. The flight was booked, and we were scheduled to leave the following day out of Paris.

Thomas placed a hot cup of black coffee on the yellow-checkered placemat in front of me.

"Happy Birthday, my love," he said in almost a whisper.

I smiled.

"Merci, mon amour."

"You need a gift!" he said excitedly.

"What? No, I don't. There isn't anything I need, except you."

A gift seemed a ridiculous expense, considering our weighty outlay of cash over the past two weeks. Thomas insisted and retreated to the bedroom, returning with a small brown box wrapped with a silky, chocolate-brown ribbon tied in a perfect bow. He placed it, almost ceremoniously, in front of me. On the top, the words Jared were embossed. Jared Jewelers? I didn't think there was one in France.

"What is this?" I exclaimed.

Thomas flashed me a blissful smile.

I gently untied the bow, placing the ribbon aside. Taking my time, I took off the top. My fingers trembled.

Inside was another box, also chocolate brown yet ensconced in velvet. Taking it in both hands, I carefully opened the lid. Shining back at me was a small-link silver necklace. Dangling from it was a tasteful, small opal pendant, encircled with crystals. I was stunned! It felt as if my eyes were deceiving me. A miniature Universe was nestled safely in front of me. A lump formed in my throat, tears pooled in my eyes.

Upon further investigation, I discovered that indeed Thomas had purchased the jewelry in California. And, in his hurried state to get to France, he decided to bring it along, not knowing where we would be on my birthday. What foresight. How romantic. This magic moment was one I would cherish forever.

At times, I still can't believe he did that. It was a true testament to his awareness of my years of hints — and his thoughtfulness — despite the chaos at the time.

Eve Chauvel

---

*"Since the Universe is in balance,
nothing can leave any point
without an equal something returning to it."*
— Ernest Holmes

Opal on the Mountain

The following month, I embarked on a small-group journey to Bhutan with Spirit Tours, a travel company based in Santa Rosa, California. Thomas had no interest in joining me, yet fully supported my desire to travel with the group. Considering the attire was very casual, it would not be appropriate for me to bring much jewelry. Yet, while packing, I opted to bring the opal necklace Thomas gifted me, because it was new, holding strong sentimental value. And it energetically connected me to Thomas.

At the end of our time in Bhutan, we were to scale the mountain up to Tiger's Nest, at an elevation of 10,240 feet. Several legends describe the establishment of this sacred, Buddhist site, located above the Paro Valley. It is one of thirteen "tiger lair" caves in historical Tibet. The monastery, built in 1692, is widely considered a cultural icon of Bhutan.

In preparation for the early morning, I gathered my clothes and battled in my head about whether I should wear the opal necklace or not. Yes, no, yes, no. The opal won. I decided to adorn myself with the magical specimen.

The trek was challenging. Of course, the early morning wasn't ideal for me, since I had spent a late night on the phone with Thomas. It was our first voice call in the entire eight days I had been gone from home. He informed me that Aunt Jocelyn had been in a serious car accident and was clinging to life. She was his dearest aunt, and my heart ached for him and the family when I heard the tragedy. I decided to dedicate my Tiger's Nest ascent to her. I was grateful I could walk when she might never be able to do so again.

I'm typically not an early morning person, yet I mustered the fortitude to take advantage of this, perhaps once in a lifetime, opportunity. Our bus of eager travelers headed toward the starting point, an hour away from our location.

The morning dew was still evident on the ground, and there was a gentle fog making its way down the valley floor. Climbing higher, I could see the sun peeking its way through the clouds, welcoming all the pilgrims with open arms. We were told that the morning is the best time to go, so as to avoid the throngs of tourists who come to see Tiger's Nest. Also, we were fortunate to have an opportunity to tour the interior chambers, due to our guide's personal connection with the monks who live there. Timing had to be perfect as they closed for lunch.

Most of us ascended on foot, while a few took donkeys up the most difficult parts due to physical issues. Along the way, I saw prayer flags, prayer wheels, several people humming, chanting, and singing. Our guide suggested we remain silent in walking meditation to the halfway point, where we would enjoy a meal and refreshment break.

As I climbed slowly, I reflected on how far I had come in life, all the little choices which added up to big ones. Here I am in Bhutan, one of the most magical places in the entire world! People dream about coming here — and I am experiencing it! I was enamored with the views, vegetation, and tranquility.

I'm willing to admit, the climb was tough. Thankfully, I was using walking sticks, loaned to me by my client Renee Russell. She and her husband, Tony, were avid hikers and had traveled around the world, yet never here. I was tickled by the thought that her sticks would now be infused with energy from Bhutan in the form of mud left over on the sharp points. As the elevation increased, my body was overheating, so I peeled off layers. Occasionally, I would touch the opal pendant, reminding myself that it was a tiny Universe lying upon my chest. Supposedly, I was the universe too, as Deepak Chopra reminds us in his teachings.

There was a lovely waterfall before taking the final ascent of the climb. The path went up and down a series of stairs carved into the hillside with strategically-placed logs. I stopped at the waterfall to take a video and express my gratitude. Taking in the forbidding climb ahead, I opened myself to whatever was in front of me. After a week's worth of chanting with monks and nuns, this was the culmination of the new practices I was learning. Truly, I thought I was in shape, yet this climb was taking every ounce of strength I had. My legs were going to need some TLC in the form of the hot tub with fired coals, promised to the group that evening.

The views from the top were majestic! Our group gradually gathered, snapping photos of each other and as a collective. It was time to enter the chambers, which required removing shoes and covering up exposed shoulders. My tank top would not be appropriate.

While pulling the sweatshirt over my head and adjusting the neck, I accidentally hooked the chain of my necklace — causing it to break. Watching, as in slow motion, my opal pendant catapulted through the air, bounced on the wood railing, then fell about 20 feet down to the ground below, which was covered in foliage and mud. I gasped. My pendant was gone!

The shock of that realization overwhelmed me, and I began to cry. A friend attempted to console me, then scurried down to locate the miniscule object. I feared it was a lost cause. A knot formed in my chest, almost preventing me from breathing. Tears continued to flow, hovering between gentle flowing and full-on blubbering. It was difficult to stop.

"Time to go inside the chambers." our guide, Tshering, announced.

I must admit, my attention span was short as my mind was playing the scenario over and over. Why did I decide to wear that pendant? How stupid of me to not be more careful when pulling my sweatshirt back on! How will Thomas react when I tell him what happened?

The attachment I felt for that object was significant, and 'letting go' was not an option in that moment. As our group moved from chamber to chamber, we had an opportunity to make contributions to every altar in the form of local currency. Each time, I knew the law of circulation was being put into action. Despite my continual flow of tears and mucus running out of my nostrils, I participated in the prayers and rituals our guide led us through. At times, my blubbering was ostensible. My body was trembling, overwhelmed with grief. I recall feeling as if the tears would never stop. In my mind, I repeated that objects can be replaced, people can't. Then it hit me: The opal came from the earth and it's now back in the earth, and what better place for it to land, but in the magical country of Bhutan at Tiger's Nest! *"Let go and let God."*

Our chamber experience was over and I went back to the railing where the pendant had made its exit. Tshering found me, put an arm around me and said, "You were really feeling it inside the chambers, weren't you?" I shared with him what happened to my pendant prior to entering the chambers. His soft grin and calming words soothed me. He asked me where this event occurred, then shared that he had led many tours where members had temporarily lost an object, yet found it after a short period of time.

Tshering beckoned his son and they scurried down the stairs to the earth below. Each took a stick in his hand and proceeded to agitate the foliage. The ground was murky and muddy. Several of us gathered above to watch the treasure hunt unfold. I wondered how long they would go at it before giving up. Of course, I had already let go and resolved myself that the pendant was a lovely gift to have, even if it was mine for only a short period of time.

Five minutes later, Tshering bent down and picked something up. Returning to where I was standing, he held his hand out to show me the pendant! Wrapping my arms around him I joyfully screamed, "You found it! I love you!" Without question, it was a gift of Spirit. I was astounded, as was everyone else.

Carefully tucking the pendant into a zippered pouch, I gave thanks to the Universe for the tough and invaluable lesson of non-attachment. Little did I know how I would re-live that lesson a few years later.

That evening, I was able to call Thomas and tell him I had a very exciting story to share, but it would be better done in person. He'd have to wait and wonder for a while.

Upon returning home to California, I shared what happened and Thomas was very understanding. He wasn't angry at all. He reminded me that tangible objects could be replaced but people couldn't (a reference to his dear aunt who was still clinging to life). When I described how the pendant was found, he was as awestruck as I had been.

And then he said, so tenderly, "My love, even if it were lost, that would be ok." Yet another example of how unattached Thomas was to things.

A Love Letter to Thomas

---

*"You cannot travel the path
unless you become the path itself."*
— Buddha

Our Last Year

In 2019, we traveled so frequently it felt as if the moment I got settled in after returning from a trip, I was packing to go on the next one. Don't get me wrong; I enjoy travel, and we were able to visit places and conduct "research and development" on behalf of our clients.

The year started off with a cruise over Christmas and New Year's around South America. Before we embarked on that trip, I imagined what it would be like to watch the New Year's Eve fireworks in Rio de Janeiro. This was visualization in action.

To give you some insight into how travel agent rates work. A request was submitted, then we waited for approval before moving forward with booking a trip. We always had the option to decline if we desired, and we had done so once in our career. This time was different and, never having been to South America, I was excited about the possibility.

We received authorization to move forward, and Thomas looked at flights. American Airlines had recently launched a direct route from LAX to Buenos Aires. We found the last two seats on that flight! Coincidentally, our clients were just finishing a one-month trek in South America that we had helped them with. We made plans to meet for lunch on the day of our arrival. It was a very special afternoon.

- In April we embarked on another river cruise, sailing with Crystal Cruises on their Crystal Bach which is considered to be one of the most luxurious river cruise vessels sailing throughout Europe.

- July brought us to Lisbon for two days prior to boarding Windstar's Windsurf for a journey to Barcelona.

- In November, we traveled to France for a family reunion. Our accommodations were the guesthouse of a medieval castle along with Thomas' brother Christophe, his wife Dawn, and their children, Morgane and Thomas. After which, we headed to Bordeaux for a one-week river cruise. There were torrential downpours and many of our excursions were cancelled. I do recall one that went as planned; a bicycle tour through the vineyards of Châteauneuf-du-Pape.

- The final trip of our year was on the Paul Gauguin, the same cruise line we had met on. What a way to end the year! After all that, I wondered what 2020 would bring.

I became a Licensed Prayer Practitioner in 2019, the culmination of two years of study. As mentioned earlier, this commitment was a colossal undertaking with a significant portion of my life dedicated to classes, writing, and homework. On page 186 in *The Science of Mind*, Ernest Holmes writes that, "the professional mental and spiritual practitioner is one who has dedicated her life, her time, her energies, her intelligence, to helping others through mental and spiritual means and methods." Little did I know that I would need to strongly employ the tools I gathered and the skills I learned in just over six months' time.

I was fortunate in that Thomas was so giving and kind in terms of supporting our household activities. He enjoyed being in the kitchen and cooked dinner for me almost every single night. He also did the dishes! My typical MO was to go to bed with a clean kitchen; his was to clean up in the morning. I was grateful for that, and thought to myself, if I wanted it differently, then I could clean the kitchen.

We enjoyed our meals in front of the television, watching shows like *60 Minutes, CBS Sunday Morning, This Is Us, Jeopardy, Wheel of Fortune, NCIS,* and movies on Netflix. In early 2020, we binge-watched the show *Dead to Me.* The story revolves around two grieving women who bond during therapy. One is a widow whose husband was hit by a car while he was jogging and the other, unbeknown to the widow, is the woman who was driving said car.

"Do you know what causes wind? High pressure meeting low pressure. Warm meeting cold. Change. Change causes wind. The bigger the change, the stronger the wind blows."
— *Mitch Albom*

Winter in Park City

On January 26, 2020, the helicopter in which retired MBA Player Kobe Bryant was traveling, along with eight other people, crashed, killing everyone on board. This event was announced by Senior Minister Jim Turrell at OC Spiritual Center's Sunday service. The congregation immediately went into prayer.

Over the coming days, Thomas and I had multiple discussions about death and dying.

"If you had a choice regarding how to die, would you want a long, drawn-out illness or a fast death? Quick and easy. Lights out."

"A fast death," Thomas answered matter-of-factly.

Our four-year wedding anniversary was approaching, and we began planning a three-day trip to Park City, Utah to go skiing. We had skied together once previously and had the great fortune of staying in a condominium belonging to our friends, Lori and Paul Curtis. It was a 10-minute walk to the Park City Resort. Unlike our last visit there we decided to fly instead of drive. It was more efficient that way.

Truth be told, I wasn't pleased about the plans when I saw what the weather would be like. Skiing in extremely cold weather is undesirable to me. Yet my heart wanted Thomas to be happy and it was a treat to see him overjoyed with the idea of spending three days on the slopes. He promptly called his friend Sam, an avid skier.

"We are going skiing! For three days!"

"Fantastic! Let's plan a trip to the local mountains this season," Sam suggested

"Oui, I am buying proper ski clothes and goggles." Thomas responded

"What about equipment?"

"We can rent those things. No need to spend the money." Thomas responded.

Not only was Thomas already envisioning the guys' time on the slopes, but Thomas and I also talked about incorporating skiing into our future travels. This would expand our horizons and allow for new opportunities to explore the world's mountaintops, despite my aversion to cold weather. After all, life is an adventure. Might as well embrace what we can, while we are still able to do so.

Coincidentally, Bruce Holler, the son of a congregant at our spiritual center, Gloria Holler, was also going to be in Park City during the same time. Bruce and his wife Virginia own a condo there, so we made plans to see them at some point for nibbles and wine. I had been working with Gloria as a Prayer Practitioner on a weekly basis for quite some time. She was a resident of an assisted-living facility in Newport Beach. Truthfully, known for her spunkiness, not many people enjoyed being around her. But I found it an honor and a privilege to sit with her, week after week, listening to her stories and praying for her well-being. She traveled to Alaska under the guidance of Dr. Jim Turrell. There were eight of us on that trip and we sailed aboard Regent Seven Seas Mariner, a ship on which Thomas had once worked. Coincidentally, a former colleague of his, Laksman Rohana, was the Sommelier on board.

A Love Letter to Thomas

Delta flight #1949 departed John Wayne Airport on Tuesday, February 4th at 10:25am, scheduled to arrive in Salt Lake City at 12:15pm. When we boarded the plane, I found myself in the middle seat, the filling in the 'Oreo cookie' of Thomas and a middle-aged Persian woman. Her smile was warm and her demeanor inviting. I introduced myself and we struck up a conversation. She was heading to Salt Lake City to visit her daughter for her birthday. A delightful reunion was to occur. As it turned out, we would be on the same flight returning to Orange County. I was eager to share with her the outcome of my anniversary trip, and we planned to find each other at the airport.

Picking up a rental car, we drove the distance to Park City, stopping at the market and liquor store for wine. The weather was quite cold and snow was predicted. A quick stop for lunch before settling into the condo gave us a short respite to take in the scenery and make plans for our coming days.

On the morning of our anniversary, the weather was predicted to be cold. We made our way to Jake's Ski & Snowboard Rental which our friends, Lori and Paul, had referred us to. I could already sense that the gloves I brought would not be warm enough. After a few runs, the numbness in my fingers forced me to return to the pro shop and find an alternative. My digits were seriously cold. Handing over almost $100 seemed outrageous, yet I figured my comfort was more important than the cost. Handling ski poles with frost-bitten-like fingers was not ideal.

Riding on the ski lift, legs dangling with the weight of our boots pulling tendons taut, we absorbed the serene scene: pine trees, fluffy snow mounds below, and occasional shouts of excitement from skiers as they traversed the hill. Despite several years having passed since our last ski adventure, our muscle memory kicked in easily. My heart seemed to beat more rapidly as the exit ramp appeared on the horizon. Pushing off the seat, I flowed easily off to the side. Whew! First major hurdle accomplished! Our initial run seemed to be easy. Thomas was in heaven, taking to the slopes as if he was a pro. Always ahead of me, I relished in the delight of watching my husband shine, joy-filled, one with the mountain.

There is nothing better than seeing my husband happy, I thought to myself.

With each subsequent run, our skill level increased. The skiing was enjoyable, very freeing. Swish, swish, swish, we glided down the hillsides, traversing back and forth. Each with our respective pace, the freedom of letting go took over. An occasional black diamond run appeared on our radar; we embraced the challenge. Jumping over moguls had been a favorite when skiing in my youth, despite not being considered a snow bunny like some of my friends. Even now, pushing the limits was exhilarating!

Back at our condo, Thomas, who thoroughly enjoyed cooking in as it was cost-effective too, prepared a delicious, simple meal for us; pasta with sausage and kale along with a nice bottle of wine. We ate at the kitchen bar. As he did the dishes, I curled up on the sofa and read.

Our second day of skiing was one that would go down in the history books. Blustery winds with even cooler temperatures than the day before, we set out for another adventure. Often, when walking around our community at sunset, which we did almost every night we were at home, I would ioccasionally joke about what it would feel like to find a $20 bill lying on the ground. I mean, wouldn't that be fantastic?

A Love Letter to Thomas

The sunlight was waning and weather getting colder. Our last ski run of the day together, we were on a wide swath and there it was: a $20 bill rolling gently down the hill, being caressed from one side to the other by a gentle breeze.

Shifting left, the blades of my skis came to a halt. Piercing the paper with my pole, I shouted to the three people passing by. "Is this yours?" Heads shook no, to my amusement. Who would turn down a $20 bill? Bending down to pick it up, Thomas said, "I'll use it to buy you a beer when we're done." Deal.

My body was aching. Fingers chilled, ankle swelling, my desire was to call it a day.

"My love, I want to rest. You can take another run, and I'll wait for you by the ski rental return."

Planting a wet kiss on my lips, Thomas smiled. "Merci, mon amour." He whisked off to catch his final run of the day. I have often wondered what he was thinking about during that run. He had a deep appreciation of nature so, perhaps, he was connecting to it on an expanded level while on this solo journey.

Do you know the feeling of taking off ski boots after a long day on the slopes? I wonder if that's how astronauts feel when landing on Earth, after experiencing zero-gravity for days at a time. The thought crossed my mind about how my aching body would feel skiing the next day, anticipating our third consecutive day on the slopes.

There was just enough time for us to walk back to our condo, freshen up, and head to Bruce and Virginia's condo to reconnect. Walking down the street towards oncoming traffic, I found myself silently wondering, *Why does Thomas insist on being on my left? When will he learn that the rules of etiquette call for a man to be on the woman's side where he can protect her from traffic?* I had noticed him consistently doing this over the years. Whenever I asked about this ongoing habit, he didn't have an answer. He had no clear understanding or explanation, even for himself. For him, it just felt right. Categorically, any time we were walking together he was on my left: at the grocery store, during our sunset walks, at the movies, touring small villages, hiking, etc. To my mind, it was odd, to say the least.

The slick sidewalk glistened from intermittent street lighting. I wondered how drivers could see in these conditions — particularly during a snowfall. We arrived at Bruce and Virginia's home and were welcomed with a lovely spread of appetizers, then offered a glass of sauvignon blanc. The conversation was lively, exchanging stories of travel, food, our Spiritual Center, and entertaining stories of Bruce's mom Gloria. We recalled our time with her on the Alaskan cruise, how it started off with her being locked out of her room and panicking. Thomas, the constant thread of calm, had been able to rectify the situation easily. Gloria was fun to travel with, a wonderful mix of cantankerous behavior and excitement about the adventure. Bruce suggested that this was Gloria's last trip as 90 years of life was wearing on her.

It was time to say goodnight and head back to the condo. Not sure what we would have for dinner, suggestions were made about which restaurants to eat at. Thomas thought we could have leftovers, as he preferred to stay in and be cozy. He almost never wanted to eat out, thinking it was a waste of money. He could prepare something equal in quality, or even better, with the proper ingredients! Besides, the markups on wine were outrageous in his opinion. It was better to stay in.

Heading back, the street was dimly lit, no change from earlier. We noticed snow banks and rugged gravel. There were no sidewalks on this side of the street. I thought, *The city must do something about this.* Staying to the right as far as I possibly could, I stumbled over the berms as we made our way back on the short walk to the cozy condo. Tripping, Thomas grabbed my hand to steady me.

"Step over here, my love, it's safer." he said, while moving slightly to the left, stepping into the gutter. The streets were vacant, not a pedestrian in sight.

Quiet. Calm. There was a feeling of peaceful serenity as we walked hand in hand, endlessly in love.

I heard a loud noise. Thud! Thomas' body flew into the air and landed about eight feet away, flat on his back with his head making a loud smack on the hard, cold, pavement. I thought he tripped on something. My body lunged forward, feet carrying me as fast as possible. My knees buckled at the sight. Blood was gushing out of all possible cavities, his nose, his mouth, and his ears. Coughing and spitting up more blood, his breathing was forced, causing bubbles to form in each nostril. The scream that came from the belly of my soul was deafening.

"Help! Help! Help!" I shrieked loud enough to cause my vocal cords semi-permanent damage. "Someone call 9-1-1!" Even with my phone in my pocket, it didn't dawn on me to make the call myself.

Blood pooled slowly behind Thomas' immobile head. He was unconscious. No movement. Labored breathing. Closed eyes. One of my favorite scarves was about to be sacrificed. I tore it off from around my neck and put it under Thomas' head as a pillow, and to soak up the blood that continued to pour out of his skull. The opening was not visible and I could see no other injuries. His beautiful face was intact, his lips quivered from the bodily shock.

I heard myself say, "Hold on my love. Stay with me." I firmly grabbed his hand and felt for a pulse. It was 50 beats per minute.

People came, the helpers. White towels appeared out of nowhere. I heard chatter. "What happened?" "Are you hurt?" Ambulance sirens harkened in the distance. As I knelt next to Thomas' unmoving body, my eyes locked with a young man crouching on the other side of his form. He looked dazed and confused. Staring as if paralyzed. More commotion surrounded me, footsteps and medical gear being unloaded pierced my awareness. The EMT's cleared a path and space around Thomas. The young man left with the crowd. *A witness, and I never even got his name.*

One of the helpers, a woman, said she was an OB/GYN. She was able to assess Thomas' vitals and report to the paramedics. I knew he was gone. Even though the lungs were functioning, it was too late, yet I didn't want to give up hope. Encouraged to step away, I rose to my feet, backed away, closed my eyes, and placed my arms along my sides. My stance was that of vertical savasana, commonly known as corpse pose.

"God, let them do what they do, and you do what you do." I whispered.

Time passed slowly. What seemed like an hour was a mere fraction of one. With Thomas' body loaded onto the gurney, the EMTs focused on me.

A Love Letter to Thomas

"Do you have a rental car?"

"Yes." Were they really expecting me to drive myself to the hospital?

"We need to take your husband to Salt Lake City. Park City Hospital does not have a Level One trauma center." University of Utah Health was approximately a 45-minute drive under normal conditions. How long would it take with the frigid temperature and snow?

"I'm going with you," I declared.

The paramedics exchanged coded conversation with each other, then escorted me to the ambulance. I overheard a witness.

"It was a van. I took a picture with my phone." said one witness

Numbness came over my body. The words didn't fully register. I wondered where the driver was.

A gentle snow began to fall. Buckling myself into the passenger seat, I finally got a good look at myself. Blood encased my black boots, my denim jeans, and new ski parka. An acrid metallic aroma drifted up my nostrils.

My intuition kicked in. I dug for my mobile phone in my pocket, then I sent a group text to my spiritual center's prayer practitioners informing them that Thomas had been hit by a car and we were en route to the hospital.

Unbeknown to me, Dr. Jim was about to teach his weekly class. Marion Whitson, a Licensed Prayer Practitioner and assistant in the class, was the first to read the group text.

"No!" she exclaimed out loud. Dr. Jim immediately led the class in prayer.

Our teaching states that speaking a desire into the creative Law has an outcome. It's simple physics of cause and effect. From my perspective, what they prayed enabled Thomas to stay alive long enough for us to get to the hospital so he could be cared for, and so I could get the support I needed from a social worker.

The snowfall became energetic. I sensed an increase of tension from the ambulance driver. Both hands gripped the steering wheel, exaggerating his knuckles and veins. He exchanged coded communication with the team in the bay where Thomas was clinging to life. My head bowed in constant prayer, hopeful we would get to the hospital safely.

"Why aren't the sirens on?" I asked the driver.

"We keep them silent when we're driving on the freeway." he said solemnly.

For some reason, I didn't believe him. Typically, I would fact check. Commotion ensued from the back. It took all my strength to focus on prayer and not get distracted.

"I'm here, my love. Hang on. We're on our way to the hospital."

Upon arrival, I was greeted by a social worker, Drue Didier, who led me inside.

"Where is the bathroom? Can I please have some water?"

After emptying my bladder, I looked in the mirror.

Bloodshot eyes stared back at me. Dry, ink black mascara streaked my face. A feeling of dread came over me. What on God's Earth was going on? Just keep praying, just keep praying.

Returning to the holding area, just outside the emergency room, someone handed me a bottle of water. I slowly lowered myself onto the cold, stiff, stainless-steel chair. The thin blue pad did not provide me with much comfort. My hands found themselves stroking each thigh, rhythmically soothing my nervous system. Text messages continued to come in. Dr. Jim called a few times.

More questions came my way from the nurses and social worker.

"What type of insurance does Thomas have?"

"Is there anyone you can call to come be here with you?"

Periodically, a nurse would pop out of the emergency room with an update.

"They're working on him as best they can."

"When can I go in?"

"Soon. We will let you know."

I continued to drink my water and observe my surroundings. I wondered how many people before me had been in this position, witnessing severe trauma and doing their best to stay stoic. I must have been quite a sight in my disheveled state: blood-stained boots, jeans, and jacket....

Minutes felt like hours. Realizing I didn't have a

phone charger with me, I turned my phone onto low battery mode. It was nearing 8:00 PM Had it only been one hour since the accident? That didn't seem possible. The door to the emergency room opened.

"Mrs. Chauvel, it's not looking good. They're working on him as best they can, attempting to restart his heart. Would you like to come in?" the nurse spoke in a soft, hushed tone.

She led me into the space. I saw what seemed like two dozen people working diligently to save Thomas' life.

"Would you like a chair?"

"No, thank you."

Moments later, I changed my mind. The staff had more on their plate than they could handle. The last thing they needed was to have me faint on the floor. I sat down.

Thomas' body was on the table, someone was standing on a step stool over his chest, working on compressions. The neurosurgeon was at his feet, hands gripped on his toes. I slowly looked around the room and made eye contact with every person I could. Equipment crowded the space; teams of people laser-focused on their tasks at hand. From my perspective, it looked like the surgeon was conducting an orchestra. He rattled off commands and questions.

"What are his vitals now?"

"Repeat the results of the CT please."

"How much blood have we given him?" I later found out the answer to that question. Eight pints.

A Love Letter to Thomas

Did you know that the human body contains eight to ten pints of blood? Privately, I made a vow to donate blood whenever I had an opportunity, despite my feeling of discomfort having a needle in my arm for the length of time necessary to extract a pint of blood.

I could sense this was the end. All attempts to save Thomas' life were failing. Again, the neurosurgeon barked off questions like a checklist of fail-safe measures, as if proving that there was nothing else that could be done.

"I'm calling it. Time of death: 8:17 p.m."

Silence fell across the room like a blanket of snow. Feet shuffled softly, machines were clicked off, and activity crept to a halt. Thomas was dead.

"Let's have a moment of silence for Thomas." the surgeon said softly.

Everyone bowed except me. I looked around and expressed an internal gratitude for their efforts. What they attempted to do was insurmountable. At least in Thomas' case. I'm confident there are miraculous stories of people recovering from life-threatening injuries. Unfortunately, that wasn't his experience.

"We will leave you alone now. Take as much time as you need." the nurse informed me.

I slowly walked over to Thomas' body. The intubation tube remained in his mouth. No life remained, only a hollow shell.

You've seen movies where the grieving person hops up on top of the body, wrapping both arms around it, sobbing, wailing, begging God to bring the person back?

That wasn't me. A peacefulness came over me. I knew that energy can never be created or destroyed; it only changes form. The human being, the substance of his soul had moved on to be something else. Standing by his left side, I gently touched his hand.

"It's still warm!" I exclaimed to what I thought was an empty room.

"Yes." the male nurse replied, as he began mopping up the room.

"Well, that's that." I said to myself, matter-of-factly. "What's next?"

Leaving the emergency room, I startled the social worker. Apparently, she had expected me to be in the room much longer. Gently guiding me down the corridor with her hand resting on my lower back, we passed by the emergency room waiting area, miscellaneous offices, ending up in a large room with a locked door. This was the bereavement room, designated for people like me. Rust colored couches lined the perimeter. The art on the walls was faded, nothing special. All I wanted to do was curl up in a ball and sleep. My contact lenses were drying out.

"I need saline solution."

"Of course. Would you like a change of clothes? We have nurse scrubs."

"No, thank you."

I was given instructions to stay there; a detective was on his way and would want to talk to me. My mind turned to the calls I needed to make.

Where to begin? Thomas' brother, Christophe, and

his family lived in Wales which was seven hours ahead. They would still be sleeping. Do I call Kelsey, my daughter? Thomas' friends? My mom? It was so confusing.

Pulling myself together, I dialed my mom's number. No answer. It wasn't too late to call, in my opinion. Really wish she would have answered. I tried again. Voice mail. Deep breaths. Focus Eve, focus. My daughter Kelsey was next. We played a short-lived game of phone tag, finally connecting. Our conversation lasted three minutes, details too raw for me to share here. What is crystal clear to me is that the news crushed her. She had witnessed my happiness firsthand, a marriage that fulfilled me completely. It all vanished in a flash. Protectively, I wanted to reach through the phone and comfort her. An impossibility. Our embrace would need to wait until I returned home... as a widow.

People came and went, most likely checking on my mental state. A basket of snacks arrived. Bottles of water appeared. It was all a blur. I continued to make phone calls.

"Is there anyone who can come be with you?" asked the social worker.

Oh shit! How was I going to get back to the condo?

I was informed that Bruce and Virginia Holler were on their way to get me. What a relief! I vaguely recall sending them a text message when the accident occurred. They had been on their way to dinner with their daughter and son in law.

Detective Darwin Little entered the room. "The driver of the van has been apprehended and is currently being booked into jail."

While I was relieved, questions still encircled my brain. Who was this person? Why did they leave the scene of the crime? What is going through their head? Do they have a support system?

Answers to these would be revealed in the days to come.

Because Thomas was a citizen of France, reporting his death to the French Consulate in San Francisco was necessary, requiring completion with the next 24 hours. I started making my list of things to do: Call the mortuary; Email Lieutenant Little a copy of Thomas' green card and driver's license; continue making phone calls.

At the end of my time with the Lieutenant, I asked if I could see Thomas one more time. The Lieutenant's eyes bulged. I sensed an urgency. Rising quickly up out of his seat, he left the room asking me to follow behind. We learned that Thomas' body was minutes away from being transferred to the morgue. We had just those minutes to get to the E.R.

The cold, cavernous space had been tidied up. Two men hovered over the grey body bag. It felt like I was walking through molasses. A hand grasped the silver-toned zipper, tugging it slowly down, stopping just below Thomas' chin. His eyes were open! What a gift! I was able to see those gorgeous, hazel-brown eyes that had expressed such profound love to me over the last seven years.

Those eyes had witnessed gorgeous scenery around the globe. They had been of service to thousands of people on cruise ships, in private clubs, in restaurants, and hotels. The world had lost one of the most generous, kind, and loving individuals ever to have walked the Earth.

A Love Letter to Thomas

My legs floated me back to the bereavement room. Bruce and Virginia had arrived to pick me up from the hospital. They greeted me with huge hugs. Disbelief was evident in their expressions.

A clipboard of paperwork was handed to me. Body release forms. Financial liability forms. The office for Victims of Crime had sent over a Victim Advocate Coordinator, Devan Bobo. She discussed my next steps for filing a claim to get reimbursement for any expenses related to the accident, including cremation of Thomas' body.

Wow! Not only was I labeled a widow now, I was officially a victim of a crime. Not a scratch on me physically. The emotional toll would come in waves, later.

I was given a new parka, mid-calf-length, black. Appropriate color for mourning, don't you think? My contacts were getting drier by the second. I was anxious to get back to the condo and throw them away.

The silence in the car was palpable. Oddly, I remember thinking, *These people are staunch Republicans from Texas. I am grateful for the ability to put any political discourse aside and focus on what is important in this moment.* Truly, I wouldn't have known what to do without their assistance.

Arriving at the condo, my shaking digits entered the code to unlock the door. Sluggishly moving down the hallway, my arms reached for the kitchen counter. Head bowed, I wailed into the space. Overcome with paralysis, my body wouldn't move. Curling up in a ball seemed like the best course of action. Clearly what my body wanted me to do. However, there was work to be done: Continue to make calls to friends and family and contact the local mortuary which I did via email at 2am.

My heart ached, knowing that the call to Thomas' brother, Christophe, was going to be challenging. Dialing the phone, I breathed deeply. No answer. I tried again. Still, no answer. I sent a direct message (DM) via Instagram to our niece, Morgane.

"Please have your dad call me ASAP."

"Okay."

The phone rang. I answered, hearing Dawn, Christophe's wife, on the other end.

"Hi. How are you?" I inquired.

"Good. The kids just got off to school. Christophe and I are getting ready for the day."

"You might want to sit down."

"Oh no, is it Bernard?"

Christophe and Thomas' father, Bernard, had been struggling with various ailments for decades. Since his wife Michele died in 2018, his prognosis had been poor. There was an increase in his use of alcohol as a result, leading many people to steer clear of his abhorrent behavior. Thomas kept in touch regularly, ensuring that the house bills were being paid and maintaining open dialogue. I remember him saying how he dreaded talking with his dad because the conversations almost always turned sour. Thomas found these conversations exhausting.

"There was an accident. Thomas got hit by a car; he died last night."

Dawn's shrieking traveled through the phone. Christophe kept repeating the word 'No' over and over. They both seemed inconsolable.

"How did it happen? Where is his body?"

I shared details of the accident, explaining that his body was currently at the medical examiner's office, and that it would be cremated in the next few days. My decision to have him cremated aligned with his wishes which had been verbalized to me during our discussions about death. The logistics of having his body shipped to California, with cremation happening there, seemed illogical. I'm a "take action" type of woman. Make lists. Set goals. Check off the boxes.

We continued to discuss the next steps, including them telling their children at the end of their school day, as well as the rest of the family.

"Christophe, please call your dad for me. My French isn't strong enough," I pleaded.

Eve Chauvel

---

*"A single person is missing for you,
and the whole world is empty."
— Joan Didion,
The Year of Magical Thinking*

Becoming a Widow

Eventually, my body gave into the heaviness of the day. Before climbing into the Queen-sized bed, I noticed something on the bedside table, to the right of the bed. It was Thomas' wedding ring! He must not have wanted to wear it while skiing. I experienced a brief flashback to our discussion about wedding rings.

Thomas had been married once previously, in his early 20's to an Australian woman. According to him, a point of contention was his wedding ring. She insisted he wear it and he refused. His reason for refusal was that it impeded his ability to execute certain work activities in a comfortable manner. Apparently, she felt that without a ring on his finger, people wouldn't know he was married.

When it came time for us to get married, Thomas wanted a simple ring, which we found at the Orange County swap meet. Costing under $100, it was exactly what he desired. Even though we exchanged rings at our wedding ceremony, I shared with him that it didn't matter to me whether he wore the ring or not, because he knew he was married in his heart. Much to my surprise, he wore his ring almost every day, except during sport activities. I remember him leaving for work at Moulin one day, returning in less than ten minutes, exclaiming he forgot his ring. That made my heart fill up with joy and tenderness. From my perspective, he was proud to show the world that he was a married man.

Snapping back to the present moment, I put his ring on my thumb, climbed under the sheets and turned onto my left side. It was four o'clock in the morning.

What happened next was astounding. An aura

appeared beside me. It was as if a blanket of stars was lying next to me in the shape of Thomas' body! His eyes blinked.

"You're here!" I exclaimed

My tears fell like a gushing waterfall.

"Why did you have to go?" I questioned through water-filled eyes. Tightly embracing my pillow, I squeezed my eyes shut. When I blinked them open, the aura had faded away.

Tossing and turning commenced. Thoughts raced between what to do next, recognizing I needed more sleep, and realizing my life would never be the same. Sleep was hopeless. The only thing I knew to do was to get ready for the day.

A shower was in order. The tepid water helped cleanse my body, temporarily washing away the sorrow of the last 12 hours. I found that sticking to my routine of getting ready for the day helped me stay focused. In all actuality, it was one of the few things I could control, leading me to remember the serenity prayer, which I learned about when attending Alateen classes in my youth.

> God, grant me the serenity
> to accept the things I cannot change,
> The courage to change the things I can,
> And the wisdom to know the difference.

Returning to my workstation in the condo's kitchen, lists of things to do strewn all over the place and Thomas' phone charging in the corner, I made myself a cup of coffee, mentally preparing for what lay ahead of me. The calls, text messages, and Facebook direct messaging continued to pour in. I was juggling dozens of heavy balls, trying my best to keep them all in the air. One of the biggest balls was authorizing the certificate for Thomas' cremation.

My phone rang, bringing me to the present. Thomas' image appeared on the screen with his name illumined across the top. Seeing Thomas' smiling face gave me a start. Was this a message from the other side?

I answered the call, curious to discover who it was. Yes, the caller ID was accurate. Just, not Thomas speaking.

"Oh, Eve", the voice laden with a thick French accent spoke sluggishly.

It was Thomas' Uncle Pierrick, calling from La Poterie, the village located in the Brittany region of France where Thomas grew up. Pierrick was the youngest of Thomas' three uncles, a chain-smoking, retired bachelor, living life on his own terms. This man had been Thomas' trusted confidant and always willing to open his home when Thomas returned from his travels around the globe. He and I hit it off from the moment we met, with me practicing my broken French, and he, practicing his broken English. For us, smiles and laughter were the norm. He even taught me a few words in Breton, a Celtic language: Yamat for 'Cheers' and Kenavo for 'Good-bye.'

Our conversation was short, mostly filled with tears. After hanging up, I realized that in my contact form for Thomas I had designated Pierrick's land line as his home number. That's why Thomas' face and name appeared when the call came in.

———————

Bracing myself for the call to my mom I took several deep breaths. Months ago, she made plans to travel to California from Washington State for her annual visit, due to arrive the following day in San Diego. I was confident her last-minute packing and planning was consuming her time. I dialed her number.

"Hi, Eve dear."

"Hi, mom. I tried to call you last night." My frustration was coming through.

"I know. I saw you called and thought, 'Well, she and Thomas are skiing. One of them probably broke an arm. I'll talk with her tomorrow.'"

"I wish it was a broken arm. You'd better sit down."

Despite my mom being quite hardy, independent, and courageous, I knew this news would be heavy and turn her world upside-down. She was very fond of Thomas and appreciative of his doting over me, which she witnessed first-hand when we visited her one year for Thanksgiving. Thomas delighted in preparing his first turkey, brining it overnight to seal in the moisture.

"Mom, Thomas was in an accident last night. He died."

She let out a shriek.

"Oh my god! Oh no! What happened?"

I proceeded to share some of the details with her,

knowing that whatever I divulged would be repeated to extended family, friends, and even strangers. That's how my mom rolls. Open shares with limited filters. My words needed to be carefully constructed. Our previously-made plans were altered; she would stay with a girlfriend, and not at my home when visiting. Our time together was going to be drastically different than initially forecast.

The doorbell rang, interrupting our conversation. Closing out the conversation, I then clumsily made my way to open the door. Scott and Michelle had arrived. Scott wrapped his arms around me and was sobbing uncontrollably. As we hugged each other, I inhaled and exhaled deeply, knowing that this was difficult for him: One of his close buddies, occasional tennis partner, and travel companion had just left the planet. They would never share a beer together again after a tennis match, reminiscing about the state of the world, while their hearts and bodies cooled down from the physical exertion.

"It's so good to see you. Thanks for coming."

When I called Scott to tell him the news the previous night, he and Michelle insisted that they come to Park City. While I was hesitant for them to show up (I knew I wouldn't have time to entertain guests), it gave me comfort to know my spiritual family was there for me. I sensed their distress and guided them gently into the living room where we could sit down.

"Let me make a call," I asserted.

After dialing a number in my contact list, the phone on the other end rang two times before the call was answered.

"Hello there." I heard with a tone of gladness.

"Hi Dave. How are you?"

"I am well. It's great to hear from you."

"Thanks. I'm calling because I have an urgent prayer request."

Dave Friedman is a Licensed Prayer Practitioner at the Center for Spiritual Living, Capo Valley in San Clemente, California. He and I have been friends for a few years, becoming acquainted for the first time when we were travelers on a tour to Bhutan, booked through Spirit Tours.

"OK. You know how I enjoy being put on the spot." Dave said jokingly.

"Well, as of last night, I am a widow." There was complete silence on the other end. I could hear the air leave his lungs.

"I'm sorry to hear that," Dave responded compassionately.

Without going into details, I requested a prayer from Dave explaining that my friends were here with me and we could all use support.

For those of you unfamiliar with the type of prayer that the Science of Mind philosophy suggests, let me explain. First, we do not believe in beseeching God for ANYTHING. Our style of prayer is labeled as an affirmative prayer or spiritual mind treatment. We are declaring that something is happening right now, in the present. All prayers align with seven principles. They are Love, Light, Life, Peace, Beauty, Joy, and Truth. Here is an example, written by me, and presented at O.C. Spiritual Center on

A Love Letter to Thomas

May 24, 2020, just 108 days after Thomas died:

> There is One Creative Power which is the Source of all life. This power is intelligent and only creates with a pure purpose in addition to a loving intention.
>
> I am one with this Source for all eternity. It moves in and through me as a guide to attaining a greater sense of good, peace, and harmony. This is the truth. I embrace it wholeheartedly.
>
> Daily, I watch my thoughts and actions, allowing them to lead me down a path that expresses my true nature. I dismiss any idea of lack or limitation while aligning myself with unwavering spiritual truths. Confidently, I approach the unknown from a position of ease and grace. Life unfolds flawlessly right here, right now. I am perfect, whole and complete just as I am.
>
> With deep gratitude, my heart opens wide to say yes in trusting that all is well. Thank you, God for permanently loving me unconditionally and supporting my life in exquisite ways.
>
> I now release my word to Law, inspired by Divine Love and watch, as my declaration becomes form.
>
> AND SO IT IS!

After the phone call with Dave, there was a knock at

the door. Virginia had come by to pick up my blood-stained clothes, offering to clean them. Generously, she also delivered soup for lunch. While warming it up in the microwave, I noticed an aura again, about four feet long, perhaps 12 inches high, hovering between the kitchen counter and ceiling.

"Does anyone else see this?" I inquired.

"Nope," was the response.

"There is an aura of some sort up there. Like this." I raised my arms up to a 45-degree angle, wiggling all ten fingers, moving my hands right to left a few times, simulating movement in the air.

"It's probably because the microwave is old." Scott retorted. I thought otherwise.

Was it just me who was seeing this? Was I losing my mind? Internally, I felt as if my connection to the spirit world had been strengthened because of witnessing Thomas die. Over the years, I had read multiple stories concerning people's spiritually becoming enhanced after experiencing a tragedy, such as the death of a loved one or near-death experience. Perhaps this is what was happening to me.

I was grateful to have such a strong support system with me in these beginning stages of my grief journey. Scott and Michelle were staying at a local hotel and offered to take me to dinner that night. We dined at an Italian restaurant in downtown Park City, sipping on a luscious bottle of red wine. Stories of Thomas were shared, including our trip to French Polynesia in December 2019, sailing aboard the Paul Gauguin. The purpose of that trip had been for Scott to surprise Michelle with an engagement and marriage ceremony. Thomas worked with the crew on board, many of whom he knew from his years working on board, and we pulled off a magical experience. I found it ironic that the ship Thomas and I met on was the ship same ship on which we took our last cruise together.

Scott generously offered to take care of returning my rental car to the airport. That took another weight off my shoulders. Our discussion touched on planning a Celebration of Life, not a dour, black-themed, gloomy event. Thomas wouldn't want that. His life needed to be celebrated in a joyous fashion. With my background in event planning, the wheels in my mind spun like a top out of control.

Before heading into the condo, Scott turned to me.

"Can we go see where Thomas got hit?"

"Sure," I responded, though inwardly reluctant.

How was I going to feel, going back to the scene of the crime? It was dark now, with the conditions being very similar to those just a mere 24 hours before.

The three of us walked to the area where Thomas' body had lain, clinging to life. We embarked on our own investigation, scouting the area for video cameras, taking pictures of the scene, and analyzing the lack of light available.

"There is no sidewalk where you were walking, is there?" Michelle questioned.

"Nope," I said firmly.

I took it upon myself to walk the steps again,

illustrating to Scott and Michelle the path Thomas and I had taken. Our last walk together, hand in hand.

No conclusions were made in our self-directed investigation. Scott took photos, I made mental notes of what to share with the detective, and then we decided to call it a night. Little did I know, this story was being broadcast far and wide. Viral media. My ten minutes of fame?

With the evening ending, one task was overtaking my mind. Packing the suitcases. My Delta flight #1056 was scheduled to depart Salt Lake City the following day, February 8th, at 2:15pm. There was plenty of time to pack in the morning, I told myself, if only I could get some sleep. The old saying, 'I'll sleep when I'm dead,' came to mind. Emotionally and physically exhausted we all needed sleep.

Goodbyes were said. A pick-up time was identified for the next day. Internally, I was anxious to get back to the comforts of home. The small cottage that Thomas and I had shared, a mere 750 square feet, one block from the beach, would be the secure environment I needed to feel safe at this time.

Thankfully, I was able to sleep for a solid six hours. Opening my eyes while still lying in bed, I stared into space. "No one is going to do this for me. It's only going to get done if I move." It felt as if my hands and feet were being weighed down by cinderblocks.

Into the bathroom I went, placing Thomas' toiletries, one by one, into his travel case. Shaving cream, razor, toothbrush, toothpaste. The deodorant was next. Snapping the cap off, I brought it to my nose and inhaled deeply, a pleasant aroma. The Gillette cool-wave scent overcame my olfactory receptors, lingering for a few moments. Why was I packing these things up? They would never be used again, at least not by Thomas.

Next, his suitcase. Hands trembling, I proceeded to methodically fold his boxer briefs, pants, shirts, sweaters, and socks. No shoes to pack. His well-loved Cole Haan tan leather lace up sneakers I bought him for Christmas, two months ago, along with what else he was wearing during the accident, were being kept for evidence at the Park City Police Department. So was my favorite scarf.

My suitcase was easier to pack. I was on auto pilot. Emails flooded my inbox, my phone rang relentlessly, and text messages pinged almost every second. I was grateful for the attention and care, knowing that in the coming days my support system would be what I relied on to help me survive each day. One day at a time.

One final task to complete before I left the condo; to write in the guestbook. I hadn't done so on our previous trip. This time, I knew it was important to get my thoughts down and express my appreciation to Paul and Lori for generously opening their condo. Little did we know this celebration would become a tragedy. The phone rang, breaking my concentration.

"I'm on my way. Be there in about ten minutes," Scott reported.

"Great! See you soon."

I collected my belongings. The heaviness of the day continued to weigh on me. One step at a time. Stay focused. Keep breathing. Scott arrived solo. Michelle had decided to stay in, curled up in bed with the blanket over her body. I could sympathize. However, I didn't have time for that luxury and longed for the day when I could. Outside, the weather was brisk with cotton like puffy clouds blanketing the sky. The occasional ray would break through, a reminder that the sun is always shining, no matter what. Sometimes it's just blocked by the clouds.

Luggage in the car. Slamming the door closed. The engine hummed in a meditative manner. We headed down the mountain toward the airport in Salt Lake City.

"Thanks again for taking me to the airport. I couldn't stay here another day."

"Glad I could be of service," Scott affirmed.

"Alright. Let's get to work. I need to plan a Celebration of Life," I said excitedly.

Looking at my calendar, I found the date: Saturday February 29th. Yes, it was Leap Day and the universe had, once again, conspired perfection. There would be no annual remembrance of the celebration, rather every four years. I began throwing questions out.

"Where should we have it? What time of day? Who could speak?"

Scott patiently listened to my barrage of questions, thinking out loud, and drawing conclusions. I was in party planning mode and the ideas just flowed.

One of the first dozen people I had contacted after Thomas died was Laurent Vrignaud, proprietor of the French bistro, Moulin, in Newport Beach. He and Thomas had grown close over the years. I appreciated how he had provided Thomas with a taste of home by hiring him to work at his restaurants. I sent Laurent a text. We agreed to meet on Monday to discuss the celebration, planned to occur at Moulin, in San Clemente, overlooking the ocean. So perfectly apropos.

It dawned on me, as the scenery whipped past my window; this was the last road Thomas drove down. Well, not really drove, as he was a passenger in the ambulance. But you get what I mean.

Eve Chauvel

"Of course I'll hurt you. Of course you'll hurt me.
Of course we will hurt each other.
But this is the very condition of existence.
To become spring, means accepting the risk of winter.
To become presence means accepting the risk of absence."
— Antoine de Saint-Exupéry,
Manon, Ballerina

Going Home, Alone

Arriving at the airport, I inhaled deeply, not knowing what I would encounter on this part of my journey. It seemed like a daunting task, traveling solo as a widow. I had traveled solo plenty of times before, yet now my demeanor was dramatically different. Scott unloaded my luggage, gave me a warm hug, and wished me a safe journey. Gripping the handles of the suitcases I walked with determination toward the ticket counter. My mind was already made-up to request that, even though my extra ticket would not be used, I did not want a refund, nor did I want another person sitting next to me.

"Checking in?" the attendant asked.

"Yes. I also have a ticket that will not be used."

She was of average height, hair slicked back in a bun, wearing red framed eyeglasses.

"Oh? May I ask why?"

With all the strength I could muster and holding back the tears, I shared with her what had happened to my husband. Her face turned ashen, and her hands began to tremble. Understanding of my situation, she was accommodating and kind. Boarding pass in hand, I expressed my gratitude, gave her a wink, and headed towards the security line.

It was a strange sensation navigating the airport in my dazed and confused state. I'm typically very savvy when it comes to travel, yet at this point I felt like I was walking through molasses. Noises were muffled. Onlookers seemed to stare at me. Grateful for my dark sunglasses that hid my puffy, red eyes. Why did I bother putting on mascara and eyeliner? I mustered down the corridor, knowing my soul would not feel safe until I was back home in my cottage by the sea.

Boarding time was about 20 minutes away. I situated myself on the perimeter of the crowd gathering at the departure gate. Thoughts danced around in my mind. Really, I'm a widow? What kind of food should we have at the celebration? What am I going to do with all of Thomas' belongings?

Out of the corner of my eye, 20 feet away, a woman was waving at me. My body turned to the left looking behind me thinking she was trying to get someone else's attention. To my surprise, she began towards me.

"Eve! Hi! How was your ski trip?" It was the woman who sat next to me on the plane from Orange County.

I froze. She glanced around.

"Where is your husband?" she inquired.

"He's not here," I responded obliquely.

"Why? Did you two get in a fight?" Her tone was sarcastic.

On our flight from Orange County, she had observed the love Thomas and I shared. The idea of us getting into a fight was extremely far-fetched.

"No. I need to tell you something. Brace yourself. There was an accident. Thomas got hit by a car. He died." I said bluntly.

Her attempt at holding back screams failed. Several

people turned in our direction. Holding out my arms, I enveloped her in a hug. She cried. I cried. Two somewhat strangers connected via grief. Grief and sorrow are two types of glue which hold us together as humans. We stay bonded as a result. The voice overhead beckoned, giving me an excuse to break away.

"Now boarding flight #1056 to Santa Ana."

We lined up, ready to board. The stares kept coming. Whispers were overheard. My seat was in the last row, window seat. Thomas would have sat in the aisle, always his preference. Long legs needed stretching room. My carry-on bag, purse, and jacket landed softly next to me. Looking around, I noticed a young family, one row up to the right. Mother, father, and small girl. Suddenly, there was a figure looming over me.

"Mrs. Chauvel?" the man asked.

"Yes?"

"I am the captain of this plane and, on behalf of the crew, wanted to express my condolences for your loss." He spoke with sincerity, while extending his hand.

Words escaped me. I was flabbergasted. All I could muster was a meek thank you. I grasped his manly, weathered, slightly hairy hand. The warmth of his palm energized me. Spirit was working through him. Another indication that we are all connected.

One by one, the entire crew visited my row. It was difficult to hold back the tears. Lips quivered. Hands were shaken. Despite my discomfort, I appreciated their kindness. Finally, the last member of the crew leaned over to me.

"When it comes time for the beverage and snack service, I'm happy to give you whatever you want first, even though we start at the front of the plane."

"Oh, that is very sweet of you. Thank you."

Actually, the last thing I wanted to do was to eat. My phone buzzed, alerting me to an incoming text. It was my daughter, Kelsey. She confirmed that she would be picking me up upon arrival. My anxiousness increased, enhancing the sounds around me. Engines whirred. Cabin doors smacked shut. Fasten seat belt indicators chimed. Ready for take off.

As the plane smoothly ascended, my eyes focused on the scenery below. Knowing I would most likely never return to this part of Utah. However, if I did, it wouldn't be the same. My ears picked up sounds of a video game. Annoyed, I glanced in the direction of the young family. Their daughter held a device with both hands. My annoyance increased. "Why can't she put headphones on," I grumbled to myself. Finally, leaning over, I was able to get the mother's attention.

"Could you please ask your daughter to turn down the volume?" I snapped.

The mother acquiesced.

Turning back towards the window, I settled myself. Breathe, Eve. Just breathe.

Time seemed to speed by. Regretting my terse tone towards the mother, my hands fumbled for a paper and pen. I would write her a note:

"Please accept my apologies for the harsh tone I

used with you. My husband died two days ago. I am not acting myself. Please forgive me."

Leaning over, arm outstretched, I got the woman's attention. She snatched the note out my hand. Her eyes looked blankly at the paper. No further interaction. I suppose I was expecting a response. Even after the plane landed and we gathered to depart, no words were exchanged. I often wonder what was going through her mind. Perhaps playing out a scenario where her own husband would die, leaving her to raise their daughter alone.

I had another long walk, navigating the airport corridor, a wide swath of people in front of me. It was surreal as I noticed their bodies were parting like the Red Sea, removing all obstacles in my way. Excited to see Kelsey, I anticipated our embrace. My baby. Someone I had comforted over the years throughout her time of need, particularly during my role as a single mother. Sharing custody of her with her father, she would often return to my house in a different frame of mind, in need of comfort. The blue and white overstuffed armchair situated in the corner of our apartment's master bedroom provided a safe space. I dubbed it the 'snuggle chair' and she and I curled up there frequently. We shed many tears while my arms enveloped her, a reminder that my unconditional love was always available. Now, it was Kelsey's turn to comfort me.

Slow-moving escalator steps in front of me. Right hand grabbing the black, slightly sticky rail. My eyes focused on the crowd below. There she was! My daughter was pacing back and forth, awaiting my arrival. Lunging forward even before the steps retracted at the bottom, I fell into Kelsey's arms. Tears and more tears.

Arriving home, I was greeted by a lovely sight. My neighbor, Maile Busby, had beautifully arranged the flower arrangements that were delivered to me over the last few days. A lantern with a lit candle added an elegant touch. She knew of my fondness for candles. In fact, I often joked about being a candle-holic. Additionally, she provided me with two bags of groceries which I found her unloading in my kitchen. The consummate busy bee, Maile gave me a quick hug then sped onto her next task.

Quite frankly, I could understand her seeming avoidance of this dance around grief. She herself had been widowed many years ago and, from my perspective, was triggered by this recent event. She adored Thomas. His loss would leave a small hole in her heart. I was grateful for her support and contribution to my immediate well-being. Another angel in disguise.

Kelsey helped me roll the bags into my bedroom. I stared at them: dark blocks, innards filled with remnants of the trip, clean and dirty clothes. Unpacking them would have to wait. The feeling of dread came over me. This task would need to be done eventually, yet when? The thought of handling Thomas' belongings once again provoked my stomach to turn. A wave of nausea overwhelmed me. The taste of vomit entered my mouth. A knock at the door broke my attention.

It was Janet and Kathleen Carroll, arriving to provide me with support. For hours, the four of us sat around my white, round, kitchen table. I did most of the talking. Kelsey served snacks and beverages as needed. Topics ranged from the accident to stories about Thomas, and making plans for his Celebration of Life. Again, my spiritual foundation was tantamount to moving through the critical days ahead with grace and ease.

A Love Letter to Thomas

For years, Janet has been another one of those angels. Not only was she my teacher for two years of Prayer Practitioner training, but she also conducted several of the classes I took since first coming to OC Spiritual Center 10 years ago. We'd had the good fortune of traveling to three destinations with Sprit Tours: Bali, Ireland, and Bhutan. Having grown up in the Science of Mind philosophy, Janet had an advantage in harnessing the power of life. However, there were times where her comments reminded me to question everything, particularly limiting beliefs. One such example was when we were touring Dingle, Ireland at the end of our 10-day journey.

Recalling A Visit to Dingle

I visited Dingle in August of 2017. It is a charming fishing village, situated on the southernmost coast of Ireland. Filled with colorful shops, art galleries, and pubs, it was home for our group's last two nights. A small number of us decided to shop a bit, strolling along at our own pace. Janet and I tended to break off from the others regularly. This day was no exception.

"Wow, look at that!" Janet pointed to a brightly painted structure.

We were both in awe of the beauty, solace, and overall spirit of the village. It felt good to be walking along the charming port, taking in fresh air, and admiring the scenery.

"Wouldn't it be cool to find a labyrinth here?" I posed.

"Are you kidding me? This is a Catholic country. Why would there be a labyrinth here?" Janet spoke in a teasing tone.

A stout man, dressed in cool-weather clothing, brandishing a stylish hat stopped us.

"Hey, have you seen the church around the corner?"

He was referring to St. Mary's. We had walked by earlier, making note to return and see the inside.

"There is a beautiful garden behind that you must visit," he added.

"OK. Thank you," we said in unison.

Making a bee line up the street, we slipped around the backside and found a stunning garden. Nature was showing off. Shrubs, flowers, and trees were singing gloriously. A rugged stone wall was situated on the far side of this section, an archway cut through it beckoning for us to enter. We did just that. Much to our surprise, there was a labyrinth! Nicely manicured, yet not too pristine, it beckoned for us to enter. Only one other person was there. Birds chirped, the fragrance of freshly mowed grass entered our nostrils, and a soft breeze passed through our hair. We proceeded with the tradition of walking a labyrinth. It was magical.

"We've got to tell the others! They won't believe this!" I exclaimed. Janet nodded in agreement.

Our excitement was palpable. Returning to our hotel we opened the carved wooden doors widely. A few of our pilgrims were seated in the lobby, sipping on Irish Coffees and tea.

A Love Letter to Thomas

"You'll never guess what we found!" Janet said excitedly

Heads turned.

"What?" our friends questioned in unison

"A labyrinth. Let's go!"

Plans were made to spread the word and meet there at sunset.

Clouds blanketed the sky, gently traversing our field of view, the setting sun casting a soft orange hue over the landscape. Looks of amazement came across our pilgrims. We took to walking the labyrinth in silence, one by one. A solemn task yet done as a collective in the sacred space. Suddenly, a cackling flock of birds flew above our heads. Quickly, someone grabbed their phone to film the scene.

"Oh my God! Look! A rainbow!" several exclaimed in union, then laughed in delight.

"We haven't had a rainbow the entire time we've been in Ireland," declared Janet.

"I asked for one," said Julie.

"Where's the pot of gold?" another questioned.

"Let's go find our pot of gold," one pilgrim declared.

"We already have our pot of gold!" Janet retorted.

Giggles were heard all around.

"Yes, we have our pot of gold. WE are the pot of gold," I affirmed.

Janet had always been a source of guidance, inspiration, and unconditional love. This was true from the moment we connected when I enrolled in the class she co-taught with Rev. Carla Schiratis, mentioned earlier in this story - *This Thing Called You*, by Ernest Holmes. Because Janet grew up in the Science of Mind philosophy (her parents and grandparents were prayer practitioners and ministers) she has a unique perspective on life which I value. I have turned to her numerous times for prayer, counsel, and support. A few of Janet's regular statements, which I have adopted into my vernacular and spiritual mindset, are:

- Spirit is not bound by precedent.

- Every moment is a meditation, and every thought is a prayer.

The table continued to support my conversation with Kelsey, Kathleen and Janet, which went well into the night. The inevitable was approaching, transitioning to bedtime. Attempting slumber in the king-sized bed Thomas and I shared was a daunting task. Originally, we had a queen-sized bed in this house. Over time, it became apparent that a larger one was needed due to his height. Even though the space almost prohibited a bed of this size, we both felt that a good night's rest was more important than the leeway gained around the perimeter.

Hugs were offered and well received. Janet and Kathleen retreated into the night.

"Mommy, do you want me to sleep with you?" Kelsey asked.

A Love Letter to Thomas

"Not tonight, honey. It's my first night back and I want to be alone."

She seemed deflated with my response. Quite frankly, I wasn't ready for that level of intimacy with her. Perhaps at some point in the future, just not now. We retreated to our respective rooms. My attempt at sleep failed. Lying awake with the list of tasks to complete I was laser-focused on covering all the bases. For much of my life, I have been goal-driven and task-oriented. This circumstance was no different.

Morning came and I continued to return emails, text messages, and welcome the occasional visitor. I decided the disruptions had to stop. I thought a sign on the door would suffice. Making do with what was available, I grabbed the black chalkboard sign hanging from my bedroom doorknob. The words "Just Married" were written in white chalkboard ink. It had hung on Thomas' Vespa motor scooter on our wedding day. Used for such a joyous occasion, it became repurposed to turn mourners away from my door. Now it read "Do Not Disturb."

Kelsey and I got to task with planning the Celebration of Life. My rough list outlined the following components and continued to grow over time:

- Use the box from Smart Cremation to put Thomas' photo in

- Provide a place for people to leave notes in Thomas' memory.

- Purchase 100 copies of Dr. Jim's book "When It's Time to Leave" for everyone who attends the event. Design and print a bookplate to adhere inside.

Kelsey graciously took on the task of putting together a slide show to be looped during the event. More suggestions came.

"Mommy, do you have Thomas' handwriting anywhere?"

"Of course."

Walking over to the antique wooden cabinet, my fingers grasped the knob, pulling the drawer open. Staring up at me was the soft blue covered notebook I purchased at the Little Prince store at 8 Rue Grégoire de Tours in Paris, France. Inside, Thomas had written recipes in both French and English for most of his favorite meals that he had prepared on a regular basis. He also included Far Breton, which is similar to a dense, prune-filled flan. He had prepared this once for a potluck meal at our spiritual center. Naturally, everything Thomas brought to a potluck was well-received.

Preparing food was one way Thomas would agree to show up to Sunday services. Twice, we planned a crepe-themed event for the congregation. Thumbing through the pages, I reminisced on the experiences, recalling various aromas that filled our cottage while he cooked. Particularly the clean, slightly sweet yeastiness of bread that smelled warm, like the comfort of a patchwork quilt on a cold winter day. How I will miss those moments.

Handing the book to Kelsey, I asked, "What are you going to do with Thomas' handwriting?"

"I want to create something with it."

We tossed around ideas. My desire was to provide a takeaway that the guests could keep, a reminder of

Thomas. It came to me, out of the blue.

"Let's have reusable tote bags printed with 'Be Nice' written on it in his handwriting."

Kelsey agreed. I called Scott. He is in the merchandising business and would appreciate the order. The plans were coming together nicely. Our meeting with Laurent at Moulin was scheduled for the following day, when more of the details would be finalized.

Four days had dragged by with sleep being a distant memory. CBD syrup, ordered by Kelsey and delivered to my house, failed to work. I sent a message to my physician of 30 years, Dr. Daisy Tint. She called me immediately. The conversation was short. During it, she shared that a family member had experienced a similar sudden death, so she could empathize with me on a very personal level. Her decision was to prescribe me an anti-anxiety medication. Fortunately, sleep came to me easily after ingesting the suggested dose.

———————

Never had my sense of self been so disrupted, with my life as I knew it completely turned upside down. Navigating this journey of grief wasn't going to be easy. As the days went on, I counted them off, wondering if it would ever stop.

Each 24-hour period brought me closer to significant firsts in my life. The first Valentine's Day as a widow was just around the corner. Not a label I was prepared to wear in the moment.

The week leading up to the Valentine's holiday quickly filled up with various activities/tasks. Kelsey and I planned to make a quick stop to see the fellas Thomas played soccer with. That was a difficult endeavor. They had become as close to each other as brothers; a diverse group, yet Thomas had fit right in immediately. His closest friend, Jim Rothwell, had been extremely distraught the night I called to tell him that Thomas had died.

A Love Letter to Thomas

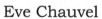
Eve Chauvel

"Love is energy."
— Marianne Williamson

Valentine's Day Eve

I was alerted that Thomas' ashes would be delivered via U.S. Postal Service between 8:00 AM and 3:00 PM — a final reminder of the human form's impermanence. As with most of Rev. Janet's statements, I fully agreed with her outlook regarding what to do with a body once it's finished with this life: cremate it. Burying a body in a casket seemed wasteful in many ways. Land is best used for the living, not the dead. I was certain Thomas would agree.

The doorbell rang. My postman appeared looking quite solemn.

"I have a package for you." His eyes darted, struggling to look directly at me.

Emblazoned on top was a red sticker, with 'CREMATED REMAINS' written in bold, block, white letters. I reached for the box. My arms collapsed from the weight — heavier than I anticipated. But seriously, how would I have known how heavy this would be? It was exactly ten pounds according to the note written on the shipping label.

I found myself wondering what else weighed ten pounds. How about a bag of potatoes? A full-grown house Cat? A large pumpkin?

Ashes to ashes, dust to dust. Now what?

I recall Thomas saying he never wanted to have his remains stored in an urn and placed on a mantel. That thought never crossed my mind. I was sure Spirit would guide me on what to do when the time was right.

Receiving the box prompted me to move forward with unpacking his suitcase. Yes, exactly two weeks had elapsed, and it was time to do the deed. The black rectangular container on wheels had been staring me in the face every time I entered my bedroom. It was situated on the camel colored, tufted leather footstool at the end of the bed.

Parts of me just wanted to throw the entire thing out without a second thought. Other parts wanted to savor every morsel of Thomas that was tucked away inside. Questions swirled in my head with the force of a cyclone. What clothes should I hang onto? Is it best to wash them first? Do I put them away in the closet or donate them immediately? Since I was planning on doing more laundry soon, I decided to throw them in with my load. Finally, the only toiletries I kept were a small pair of grooming scissors and a styptic pencil.

Another major event on this day was to share Thomas' passing with our clients. Sitting down at my computer, my fingers were guided to write the following:

Dear Friends,

It is with a heavy heart that I share this news with you. My beloved husband and business partner passed away on February 6th as a result of injuries sustained when a vehicle hit him while we were walking down the street in Park City, Utah. We had experienced two epic days of skiing in celebration of our 4th wedding anniversary. This loss was very tragic and sudden, yet I'm confident Thomas was not in pain before he passed.

A Love Letter to Thomas

A Celebration of Life has been planned:

Saturday, February 29th ~ 2:00 PM - 6:00 pm
Moulin Bistro at 120 Ave. Pico in San Clemente, CA

The event is an open house format with guests coming and going as their time allows. A short program will take place at approximately 3:30pm. Please come if you feel moved and RSVP to me directly so we can have a headcount for the food.

The Seaview Voyage business will continue yet will not be the same without Thomas' incredible passion for travel and his kind heart. Serving your vacation needs is important to me and I will do my very best to continue to do so.

Thank you for your patronage and please let me know if you have any questions.

Warmest Regards,
Eve Chauvel, MBA, ACC

Selecting all clients in the database with email addresses, I hit send. Whew! Another significant task completed.

That evening, my mom and I visited Dr. Jim's Spiritual Economics class. It was important for me to continue showing her how important my community was and to honor them for rising to the occasion the night of Thomas' death. Also, I felt compelled to ensure that these people knew how grateful I was for their work. Gratitude is one of my spiritual practices. I firmly believe that the more we express our gratitude, the more we attract to be grateful for.

The administrative office was home to several of the classes I took, including my two years of Practitioner Training. I spent many hours in that space, as a regular volunteer, particularly after Amorra Rae the Administrative Assistant, passed away suddenly in 2017.

Beep beep beep. A chime announced our arrival as the door swung open. All eyes turned in our direction. It seemed as if two rows appeared, like soldiers in a formation. An over-flow of hugs came my way. With my primary love language being physical touch, the affection was welcome.

"May I address the class before you begin tonight?" I asked Dr. Jim. "Of course."

Hands trembling, I clasped them together, right thumb on top. Holding them waist high with elbows bent simulating a relaxing state, I formulated my thoughts. Paul Williams, in his book *Gratitude & Trust* shares six affirmations that will change a person's life. The one that seemed to guide me in this experience was, "I don't know how to do this, but something inside me does." This statement continues to guide me in times of challenge.

Words came easily as my intuition kicked in. Speaking from my heart, I reiterated my gratitude for their many condolences and acts of support. Again, my firm belief is that the prayers they said the night of Thomas' passing allowed him to stay alive long enough for us to get to the hospital so the medical team could attempt to save his life and I could get the support I needed.

A Love Letter to Thomas

Eve Chauvel

A Love Letter to Thomas

"*I am the dust that dances in the light.*
I am the sun that chases out the night."
— *Rumi*

Celebration of Life

The morning rays of sun raked across my bed, splintering through the cracks in my woven-wood window shades. The day had arrived. *Here we go*, I thought to myself. Upwards of 200 people had responded to the invitation. People from O.C. Spiritual Center, friends, clients, the guys from Thomas' football team, and family members, including my estranged father and his wife. I tracked all the responses on a spreadsheet and broke down the categories. My organizational skills kicked in. Years of planning fundraising events paid off.

Moving slowly, I dragged myself to the kitchen for a cup of coffee. Kelsey was already there.

"Good morning, Pumpkin."

"Hi, Mommy!"

We embraced for what seemed close to five minutes.

After reviewing the plan for the day, my attention turned towards mentally preparing for the onslaught of emotions that would surely come over me. The shower was beckoning. Self-care became more dominant during this time. Longer than usual showers allowed my body to relax, the water flowing gently down from head to toe, cleansing my flesh and soul.

I desired Thomas' Vespa to be on display. This was an important artifact, particularly for the football players, as Thomas rode it to most of the games. Many of the guys recalled how excited they became at hearing the engine's hum when it approached the field. My friend, Thomas Christensen, agreed to ride the Vespa down to Moulin in

San Clemente, where the event was to be held. He picked it up the night before, cleaned it up, and filled the tank with gas.

The family members from Wales and France were to meet me, Kelsey, and her friend Graeme at the venue. My new acquisition from Anthropologie, a colorful, belted shirt dress, was perfect for the occasion. Slipping into my black loafers with gold buckles, I recall being excited for the celebration. It was guaranteed to be a unique experience, unlike any other traditional memorial. Thoughts continued to lean towards gratitude for how all these pieces came together beautifully. My reliance on Spirit to guide me was strong. Stronger than ever.

Kelsey had worked diligently at creating the program and slideshow of images that would be looped on three monitors for the guests. Mark Wood Productions had been hired to execute the audio-visual aspects. Laurent Vrignaud, owner of Moulin, put together a scrumptious spread of quiche, pastries, and charcuterie. Wine, beer, and champagne were offered as well. No detail was overlooked.

Driving south in my black Mini Cooper on Pacific Coast Highway, I continued to be grateful for my life. The sunlight glinted off the small white cap waves like tips of meringue on a perfect pie. Calm serenity surrounded me, a reminder that peace is my greatest strength. Thomas glowed when he was around the ocean. I was glad to know that the last years of his life were spent living in one of the most gorgeous places on the planet.

Kelsey and I pulled into the parking lot. Helpers scurried towards the car, ready and willing to unload the contents. It was filled to the max with items for our celebration:

- 100 copies of the soft covered book, *When It's Time to Leave* by Dr. Jim Turrell

- Kitchen twine, mini clothespins, and vanilla colored card stock for people to write notes on and hang in a window

- A cherry wood box with Thomas' ashes securely inside, along with a photo of him on the Vespa in a frame. Patty Turrell brought battery-operated tea lights to arrange around the box, allowing people to turn one on in remembrance of Thomas.

- Cloth, reusable bags with a blue handle and the words "Be Nice" printed in blue ink, using Thomas' handwriting as the font style.

- Small tissue packs with the words "For Your Happy Tears" printed on them.

I spotted Laurent, the owner of Moulin, across the restaurant, waiving my right hand in the air to get his attention.

"Bonjour!"

"Bonjour. You're good?" Laurent stated while kissing me on both cheeks.

"Oui. Thank you for everything. It's going to be a packed house!"

"Whatever you need, don't hesitate to ask."

Laurent had been a godsend in the planning process. He and his wife Sophie were lovely people, always willing to be of service for their customers. Butterflies fluttered in my stomach, reminding me to take a minute and ground myself in the restroom. I closed the door, pushed the lock on the handle, and walked towards the mirror. Puffy eyes stared back at me. Bright pink lips curled upwards creating half of a smile. Turning inward, I continued to remind myself that Sprit was leading the way. All I needed to do was to breathe; stay focused, and be present. After a few minutes, I was ready to face the music. Literally.

People began arriving. It felt good to have everyone's love and support surrounding me. Excitement filled the air, particularly as the music began playing in sync with the slideshow of images Kelsey selected. Friends, fellow Prayer Practitioners from O.C. Spiritual Center, and family members arrived. My estranged father and his wife appeared.

"Oh Eve!" My dad said with a caring tone. We hugged.

"I can't believe you're keeping it together."

"Thanks for coming. I love you."

Our exchange was brief as I was being summoned to prepare for the formal program.

Guests began settling into their seats. It was standing room only. Family members from Europe sat aligned in a row directly in front. Sitting stage left was Dr. Jim Turrell, Reverend Janet Moore, and our friend Scott Trippanera. They would be speaking, along with our friend and client Tony Russell as well as Thomas' soccer buddy Jim Rothwell. Everyone stood like soldiers nearby. Reverend Janet was in place to kick-off the program.

When I began to plan this magnificent celebration, I

felt it was important to start out on a high note. The song "Crazy Little Thing Called Love" by Queen blared through the speakers. Then Reverend Janet began, first by thanking everyone on the family's behalf:

> "Please know with me, whichever way you know God, this Universe, the Energy, the Power, however you know God within your heart; let's just know together that there is this one mind. This one life that we are here to live and to live fully. And we are here today to celebrate the presence of Thomas. To celebrate the love that is within all of our hearts knowing that that love is what connects us all and is what connected Thomas to each one of us. So we just acknowledge that this life is here for us to live and to live fully. And we know that Thomas did this in amazing ways. He lived life fully and with a great sense of kindness and love. And so each one of us has that same kindness and love within ourselves.

> "And so I know that we move forward from this moment and we share that gift that is within our hearts and we move forward in the world in creating this world to be a better place in the way that Thomas would want us to. And so we celebrate; we celebrate that life of Thomas. We know that that life of Thomas is with each one of us always. And so it is with a great sense of gratitude that I give thanks. I give thanks for this opportunity for each and every one of us to be here. I give thanks for the presence of God. I give thanks for the connection that has been created here just by knowing Thomas. So it is in a deep sense of gratitude that I release these

words knowing it is so. And so it is!"

Holding the microphone stand with her left hand, Janet removed the microphone with her right.

"I prefer to walk around rather than stand still while talking." Her voice was calm and cool. This was her typical modus operandi.

"I want to share with you the reason for the song that we gathered to. The song has a very special meaning to Thomas and to Eve. As some of you might know, Eve loves to dance and Thomas, not so much. But Thomas loves soccer! So they didn't dance together all the time. One time, they were on a cruise and Thomas recognized the band, Siglo. He had worked with them on the m/s Paul Gauguin.

"When the band started playing 'This Thing Called Love,' Thomas grabbed Eve's hand, they ran onto the dance floor. After that, anytime they heard this song play they would get up and dance. So next time you hear that song, maybe you will think about Eve and Thomas.

"Today we are here to celebrate Thomas and to connect and heal. We are here to recognize that Thomas is no longer here in form and to recognize that life is eternal. In some philosophies, they teach that life is eternal. So too does science. It teaches that energy can never be created or destroyed. It's just the form that changes.

"Thomas brought something of value into each of our lives. Each one of our lives. Look at everyone in this room. He lives on through our thoughts, our words, and our actions. We don't want to measure a life by the days we lived, but by the lives we have touched. That's what we are here to do, is to touch people's lives. Thomas lived a life fuller than most. He did that in an amazing way.

"Some people may ask, 'Why did this happen?' The truth is we do not know, and we may never know. Thomas would want each one of us to keep on living and keep enjoying life. We can find peace knowing that there is only love and we are all connected in love."

She concluded with the following, slightly revised poem, originally written by Shannon Lee Mosely.

I'M FREE

Don't grieve for me, for I am free

I could not stay another day,
To laugh, to love, to work or play.
Tasks left undone must stay that way;

If my parting has left a void,
Then fill it with remembered joys.
A friendship shared, a laugh, a kiss;
Oh yes, these things, I too will miss.

Be not burdened with times of sorrow

A Love Letter to Thomas

Look for the sunshine of tomorrow.
My life's been full, I savored much;
Good friends, good times, a loved one's touch.

Perhaps my time seems all to brief;
Don't lengthen your pain with undue grief.
Lift up your heart and share with me,
The love and friendship I have with thee.

When Laurent sauntered up to the microphone, his demeanor was slightly tense. I'm sure that the days leading up to this experience were difficult for him.

"I started Moulin about six years ago and I didn't really know what I was doing at the time. We had been in business for about four or six months in Newport Beach. Thomas walked in and said look I'm looking for a job. I'm French. I'm a server. I'm a sommelier. Everything you do here I know how to do.' I really needed help so obviously, what he said, registered with me and the first thing I asked is, "Are you legal?" He said, "What kind of legal? Legal eagle?" I said what's your story? "I met someone on a boat, she lives in Corona Del Mar we're going to get married and then I'll be legal. I'm almost legal." I've been in America for a long time and I used to watch The Love Boat so like wow there's this French guy from Brittany, I've got family in Brittany. I completely registered to Thomas coming into us at the time when we really needed help. Right place, right time.

"Thomas worked as professional server to come and

help me out with the dinner part of the business. We bonded. It was an incredible, incredible experience. We also started talking about traveling. As I got to know Thomas, I started asking him about his experience working on boats, big cruise ships, for six years. He was in love with it! I used to tell him I can't fathom going on a boat of that size with that many crazies and all you can eat buffets. Eventually, my wife and I went on three cruises. The first destination was Cuba which is wonderful.

"What is really important about Thomas is what we did here at Moulin as a team. He, myself, and a few others. We created this brand which a lot of people locally have gotten to know. We're opening many more locations and the people that are working for me now will have an impact, but they'll never have the impact like Thomas had for us in the beginning."

The next person to speak was Valia, Thomas' cousin from Brittany. Their relationship was deep, almost like siblings.

"Hello everybody. So, my dear Thomas, I've been writing this letter on the plane since I didn't have the heart to write it earlier on back home. I know you won't like what I'm going to say but when my dad phoned to tell me about the accident, it broke my heart. I have lived all my childhood with Thomas. We were free and fearless, always ready to go on an adventure. Building huts in the woods, unaware of time passing by, and coming home to our grandparents late at night. We rode our bikes like we were invincible warriors. Nothing could stop us. I loved the feeling.

"We had so many good times together. I remember us trying to smoke toilet paper near the fireplace at our grandparent's house, pretending to be grown-ups. Or us watching Hitchcock TV series late at night and not being able to sleep anymore, because it had frightened the hell out of us.

"Thomas, you were acting bold crazy sometimes like one winter day when you decided to sled your way through the icy pond in front of our grandparent's house. God, that was dangerous! I remember when you made our grandmother go mad by jumping on your bed late at night, waiting for her to come up the stairs, turn the light on in our bedroom, while you and I tucked in our beds pretending to sleep. My God, I was afraid of our grandmother. All you did to make me laugh.

"I want to thank you for that, Thomas, because I think humor is a great way to get through life and I'm very thankful. I'm very thankful we never lost that connection as we grew older.

"But I cannot talk about our childhood without mentioning the one person you and I looked up to, your big brother Christophe. You thought the world of your brother, always wanting to follow in his footsteps. I remember the first time Christophe and his friends lit a fire in the hut. That blew our minds! These guys were our heroes and when they started to grill chestnuts and eat them, that was it. Everything they did we would try to do even if it was going swimming in the very muddy pond on hot summer days. That was bad.

"I am so proud of you, Thomas, what you became. Not only did we share the same humor, but we shared the same values that were given by our beloved grandparents. On behalf of our family and friends back in France, I can say for sure we will dearly miss you, Thomas. Your modesty and kindness made us feel loved and we will always love you back. Most importantly, our thoughts go to you, Eve, his beloved wife who contributed to his happiness these past years. Thank you all from the bottom of our hearts for welcoming us so warmly and on such short notice and giving us the opportunity to share this beautiful ceremony."

There wasn't a dry eye in the house. Following Valia was Tony Russell. Tony and his wife Renee had become good friends of ours after starting out as clients. Well-traveled individuals, it was a bit intimidating to fulfill their requests for assistance. However, over time, our confidence grew as well as their trust in us. Tony began:

"It's tough to follow Valia. Being here is a real treat. The rules came down from Eve - no more than three pages and keep it to three minutes. Well, in the run through I had to throw out all my good jokes! Hello, my name is Tony Russell, and my wife is Renee. Several years ago, our friends Tom and Robin Christiansen called me and said they met this great couple at a dinner who were travel advisors and were planning a travel presentation. So, they invited us to come. It was at Moulin in Newport Beach.

"There we were introduced to this wonderful Southern California surfer girl with an MBA who met Thomas on a cruise ship and fell in love. Two ships passing that really bumped together. That's fantastic! Who would have thought? Would you think it would work out? Well it certainly did! They radiated happiness and love. Thomas and Eve wonderfully put together this presentation on a cruise line unfamiliar to us. The problem was it was a French cruise line.

"I don't speak French and I'm frankly, foreign-language challenged. Thomas immediately said, 'That's no problem. We have both English and French cruises.' "Then he went on to say that you can also handle any cruise line for our travel needs. At that point, we were sold! In time, they arranged numerous cruises and tours including two months in South America. It was clockwork. Thomas knew how much we liked Eve so when he scheduled us to be in South America he cleverly planned for the two of them to be in Buenos Aires so we could all meet for lunch!

"In preparation for our trips, we would meet numerous times on our patio, enjoying a typical cheese and meat platter, called charcuterie. I still can't pronounce it properly. Thomas would kindly try to correct my French while looking at me in amazement, probably thinking, 'Yeah, just another American butchering this wonderful language.' It is a wonderful language.

"Thomas, as you heard, is also a home chef. On occasion, he would bring his homemade bread to enjoy with a glass of wine. When I asked if he would like another glass of wine, he looked at me in minor amazement and responded, 'I am French!' On one of our cruises, which took us along the northern coast of France, Thomas recommended several special cafes and a must-stop at a cheese and butter store, Le Beurre Bordier, in St. Malo. We bought a brick to bring back on the ship to share with others. It was delicious, so much in fact that people at our table preferred Thomas' butter and bread! What a treat! It was the best dinner we had. Our table mates couldn't get enough of that butter.

"In my opinion, Thomas was understated sophistication. He could have been a James Bond, Maurice Chevalier, or even a Francois. To me, he was Thomas. He would tell me that tomorrow never comes, with a quiet shyness and clever smile. Eve honored me by asking me to help celebrate Thomas today. Every day is a day we miss Thomas. Thank God we have Eve."

A Love Letter to Thomas

As I watched each person tell their story, my heart was filled with warmth. Snuggling next to Kelsey, I continued to feel the love that emanated through the room. It was so evident that Thomas deeply touched many lives. Some of the stories I hadn't heard, which was refreshing. Next up was Scott Trippanera.

"My name is Scott and I have known Thomas for about four years. We met Thomas and Eve through church. Most church members here kind of know Thomas. We had a chance to go on a cruise that Eve and Thomas had set up for our whole church and that is really were where myself and my girlfriend, Michelle, got to know them. We had a really wonderful trip and what was born out of that was an opportunity for Thomas and me to get to know each other after that trip. The three things that I really know about Thomas, which I'm sure you will agree with, is his passion for travel, his passion for food, and his passion for sport.

"One of the things that we agreed to do after our first cruise to Alaska is to play tennis. You know, Thomas was very humble and didn't really suggest that he knew a lot of things about tennis, but he said, 'I'm game. Let's do it!' So we played. I've been playing tennis for about 20 years, and you know I'm in my early 50's and Thomas just gets a racket from I don't know where and he shows up. The first three times we play, I beat him which is to be expected. He never got upset, he never threw his racket, he just showed up. Then, he started to win and win, and I never won again once he figured the game out.

123

I did everything I could cause you know I played.

"So that was fun. Yet I was guilty of getting upset and hitting my racket while Thomas was always calm and steady and even allowed for me to sometimes when I get a good shot past the Frenchman.

"One of the things that he would do when we would play tennis, I think this is a very French thing, is he would bring 2 bottles of beer and we would sit and we would chat and it just gave us a chance to expand our friendship and to get to know each other and there was always a mutual exchange. I always like to get to know my friends and I want them to know about me and I know I achieved that with Thomas.

"When I wanted to propose to my girlfriend, Michelle, I wanted to do it in a special way. So, I planned a trip with Thomas, asking him to please help me do a surprise engagement proposal and marriage all wrapped in one on a cruise to Tahiti. It was terrific. Thomas seemed to be more excited than I was! This love that came together to support me on what I wanted to do was quintessentially Thomas. He paid attention to every detail. Eve and Thomas went on the trip with us, they were my cohorts in this, and we pulled it off. I was gifted with this shirt I'm wearing! At the time, it was a surprise. Everything went great and just spending that time with Thomas and their friendship just bonded us even more.

"I'm grateful for Thomas and his friendship. There were a couple times, and I don't have a lot of events in my life personally, but there were a couple of times when I got too busy to meet Thomas for one of our tennis dates and it really bothered me. But Thomas was always gracious. I do regret not showing up. What I would give for a couple more volleys with Thomas. I miss him. My advice to you is, just show up."

Again, not a dry eye in the house.

Eve Chauvel

A Love Letter to Thomas

*"A great soul serves everyone all the time.
A great soul never dies.
It brings us together again and again."*
— Maya Angelou

My Turn to Speak

I hugged Scott tightly as we traded places. Adjusting the microphone, my eyes scanned the room.

"Now, it's my turn."

Silence.

"Good afternoon. Thank you all for being here and taking time out of your day to celebrate my lifetime love, Thomas Chauvel. Before I begin, let me express my heartfelt gratitude to the following people:

- Laurent for opening up his space here and donating the food.

- My spiritual mentors, Rev. Janet and Dr. Jim. I wouldn't be where I am without you.

- Bruce and Virginia Holler for coming to my rescue at the hospital in Salt Lake City.

- Scott and Michelle Trippanera for traveling to Park City & guiding me through my fog of grief.

- My immediate family who only met Thomas a few times. I'm so glad you're here today.

- My extended family from Wales and France. Your smiling faces give me great joy. I will do my best to show you Thomas' favorite places during your visit.

- Anyone who sent gifts, cards, food, and messages. Your support is much appreciated.

- Everyone who spoke here today. Thank you for your sharing your stories about Thomas.

- Last but not least, my daughter Kelsey. YOU have truly shown me what a gift you are not only to me, but also to so many others. Your unconditional love and the intuitive way you know how to comfort me in exactly the right way at exactly the right time are demonstrations of pure compassion and caring. Pumpkin, you are my rock and I love you with all of my heart.

"Every single person here is a gift to the world. In your unique way, you contribute qualities that no one else does. And just by being here, you are supporting not only me, but also everyone whose lives were touched by Thomas. He was an incredible inspiration for many and will be greatly missed. Yes, there are numerous things Thomas and I didn't get to do, but there are so many things we did get to do.

"In our four years of marriage, which we celebrated the day before he passed away, we seized every opportunity to travel! Of course, being travel advisors, we were conducting 'Research & Development' on behalf of our clients. During our marriage, we experienced ten ocean cruises and four river cruises. Not to mention the numerous road trips we took throughout the US and Europe. I'm sure Thomas would have packed more in as he was always willing to begin another adventure, sometimes even just 24 hours after returning from a trip. As he would often say, 'To travel is to live!' He was so curious about the world and he had a passion for learning about other people; how they lived, what they ate, what they drank, and seeing everything that our miraculous planet has to offer.

"Thomas experienced the world. He set foot on every

continent. Yes, including Antarctica! I believe it was his grandfather, Michel, who instilled Thomas' curiosity for geography. Perhaps now the two of them are sharing stories while they travel around the Universe with everyone else who has gone before us.

"I am fortunate to have attracted Thomas into my life. He was a quiet, humble individual who lived simply and loved me deeply. When we got married, he promised to bring me coffee in bed every day. He did that no matter where we were in the world. Thomas was generous with his time yet also mindful of having a work/life balance. He was athletic, loved afternoon naps, and enjoyed being in the kitchen. Not only did he cook dinner just about every night, he also washed the dishes. I was pampered. I was spoiled. I was loved.

"Not a day went by that we didn't say 'I love you.' at least once, typically closer to five times. Quite often, we would ask each other, 'Is there something I can do to make you happier?' I learned to say this because my belief is that as individuals we must already be in a place of such great personal happiness that our partner only enhances that emotion, rather than to become the sole source of it.

"We both embraced an attitude of gratitude and delighted in the simple moments of life such as taking in a beautiful sunset, enjoying a delicious meal, hearing the sound of rain falling on the rooftop, feeling the warmth from a fire in the fireplace, soaking in the tub together and watching Seinfeld. I loved hearing him laugh. I also loved hearing him shout at the television when Arsenal, his favorite football team, wasn't meeting his expectations. While I wasn't a big fan myself, sometimes I would surprise him by memorizing certain facts about a recent match or a player, then casually mentioning them in conversation. He would always seem startled by my interest and reward me with a big hug. There is so much more to say about him, I could go on for hours. Yet in the interest of time, I must close.

"One of the best qualities Thomas exuded was kindness. With clients, friends, teammates on the field, neighbors or even complete strangers he was always nice. While we were driving once, I witnessed him pull over and stop the car to help an elderly woman on the sidewalk who had fallen down. This is just one example of his many acts of kindness.

"So in honor of him, my daughter designed and Scott donated these tote bags with the phrase 'Be Nice.' These are special, limited edition bags and the font you see is Thomas' own handwriting. So, when you leave today, please take one and use it in remembrance of Thomas. (The 'Be Nice' bags are available on evechauvel.com)

"Oh, my love, I suppose your work here on Earth was done. It's still so hard to believe yet I know we will meet each other again in another realm. Until then, I will continue living my life to the best of my ability and be an example for others on how to just 'Be Nice.' I love you my love."

Whew! I mustered up the courage and did it. No tears. No shaky legs. My resilience paid off. Time would tell how long that lasted.

Last, but certainly not least, was Dr. Jim Turrell.

"Eve provided for you a book I wrote about four or five years ago because, as I've been a minister for 36 years, I was watching a lot of people pass away suddenly, and understanding a lot of people have a hard time with that because nobody's prepared. Nobody was truly prepared for what happened to Thomas. So I wrote a book specifically about the subject, entitled *When It's Time to Leave*. She bought 100 copies. If you'd like a copy, be sure to take one, because it will help you understand how sudden passings happen, and also it can give you the point of view which helps you be strong for others.

"One point I wrote about is that life is not a one-trick-pony. It's a process of death and when it's not aimed at peace of mind, it defaults to fear. Life is dimensional and it must be respected in all its dimensions. Those who ignore the process of life by not being proactive and procreative default to the process of death by fear and that will look like the only doorway out of the experience.

"Life is a conscious choice. It is a choice that we must make each day. The benefit of this choice is Peace of Mind or, as one might call it, the peace of God and knowing that life is an eternal experience. Choice, however, is not automatic. It must, by necessity, be made by each person each day. This is not an option, it's a requirement.

"It's hard not to notice that so many of you have made the choice to be alive, but to be alive in a very special way. To be alive as Thomas and Eve have been alive on this planet since they met each other which is this amazing combination of love and kindness. There's three words I always tell people that's sort of my mantra. I strive to be peaceful, I strive to be patient, and I strive to be kind. That is exactly the way Thomas was in my life. I'm sure everybody here noticed that.

"So part of my job today is to help bring this to completion, because we need to put a period at the end of his life here. But there's a new chapter for him and it goes on. Eternal life is absolute and we all go forward to spread beauty. In spirit and in my philosophy there is no space or time, there's just the presence in our lives, and how well we love each other, and whether or not we're focused on being loving.

"If there was a genius in Thomas, it was that he knew how to love you, but he did it in such a way that you didn't know you were being loved. He was there *in* love for you.

"So, like any passing, everybody in this room knew Thomas differently. If we could have all of you talk, we would see a more complete picture of Thomas which is quite a bit more complex than just the few who've spoken fabulously of who he was to them. In every heart in this room, there is a space which is now empty, which is Thomas.

"In real life, we are given the opportunity to take that space when it appears for us and say to ourselves that's the imprint that Thomas left in your life about how to love other people. Is there any doubt in anybody's mind here that Thomas taught you that simply by being is how you become love. So, if Thomas could say it he would say the best way to honor his life is to love each other like he loved you. Love each other like he loved you, and you can take the lessons from everybody that spoke today. It was so profound, so meaningful that you could not have missed the point of Thomas's life.

"So we're going to take a few moments to say goodbye to Thomas, each in their own way. If you want to close your eyes let's take a moment in silence to know for Thomas his ongoing perfect love in life and the goodness that he brought to each one of us."

Everyone became even more silent. We took approximately 40 seconds to turn inward. The hum of the microphone reverberated in my ear. A few people shuffled in their seats. Car keys clinked in someone's pocket.

Reverend Jim spoke softly.

"So, I want you to see Thomas dancing in your heart right now to this amazing song, All You Need Is Love, by the Beatles."

The song played in its entirety with everyone singing along. Then, Dr. Jim concluded.

"Now, to put a period on this, we're going to say we

love you Thomas, three times, starting soft and getting louder. Loud enough so the whole town of San Clemente can hear us."

We love you, Thomas.

WE LOVE YOU, THOMAS.

WE LOVE YOU, THOMAS.

"God bless you all. Thank you so much."

Applause. More tears. I could relax now, knowing that the hard part was over. People gathered around, waiting to give me a hug. What I really wanted to do was grab a bottle of champagne, head out to the beach and sit. My mind was racing.

As people began to say their goodbyes, Kelsey approached me.

"Mommy, let's go watch the sunset."

She grabbed my hand and we sauntered down to the bluff along with a few others. I'll never look at sunsets with my previous set of eyes. Forever changed, my perspective has a new depth and appreciation for the little things.

Glorious moments.

Eve Chauvel

A Love Letter to Thomas

"The clearest way into the Universe
is through a forest wilderness."
— John Muir

Thomas' Legacy

Thomas had an affinity for trees, identifying various species we encountered during our travels. He also deeply cared about the environment. I came to realize that a long-lasting way to honor him was to help improve the imbalance on our planet, because of climate change. In lieu of flowers or gifts, I suggested people make donations to the Arbor Day Foundation in Thomas' honor.

The 'Be Nice' tote bags were a huge success! I was handing them out like hotcakes for free everywhere I went. When people heard the backstory, they were in awe. This movement had legs. Working with Scott Trippanera, we launched two additional product lines: sweatshirts and face masks. Specifically, twenty gray, crewneck sweatshirts and eighty black-hooded sweatshirts, with 'Be Nice' printed in light blue ink and white, respectively. Various versions of a 'Be Nice' cloth face mask also came to fruition. Due to the pandemic, the masks were a natural progression of this creative project. My decision to order more of the masks came from a conversation with a stranger one afternoon.

I had taken myself to lunch at Nekter Juice Bar in Costa Mesa, California. Situated at a metal table, outside in the sun, nibbling on my Acai Bowl, a man looking to be in his late 50's sat down at the neighboring table. We smiled cordially at each other.

"Do you like your Acai bowl?" he asked.

"Yes. It's very healthy and boosts my immune system." I replied.

I had been on a mission to stay as healthy as

possible during the pandemic. Food is medicine. So are our thoughts.

"What does that say?" He pointed to my black face mask, folded in half to my right.

I placed my spoon down, lifted the mask with both hands, and stretched the loops over each ear, adjusting the cloth over my mouth.

"Oh, wow! 'Be Nice!'" he exclaimed. "We need to do more of that these days."

"Agreed."

Taking the mask off, I shared the tale behind its creation. The man was choked up.

"My father's name was Thomas. He died when he was also 43."

The coincidence was uncanny. I could barely respond. Words struggled to leave my mouth.

"I'm so sorry to hear that," I uttered softly.

Saying our goodbyes, I had an impulse from the Divine: Order more masks. At least one hundred of them.

Including donations and proceeds from the 'Be Nice' products, well over 800 trees have been planted in Thomas' name. That's a small forest!

Eve Chauvel

A Love Letter to Thomas

---

*"The spirit of love arranges all meetings
in divine order for the highest good
of all concerned."*
— Alan Cohen

Eve Chauvel

Closure in Brittany

Due to the pandemic, I was not able to arrange for Thomas' memorial in his home country until October 2021. Coordinating schedules can pose a challenge, and with the outer forces pushing me, something had to give. At long last, I boarded a plane from John Wayne Airport on October 22nd bound for Paris, connecting through Atlanta. Pandemic restrictions still applied — mask wearing was mandatory! I wondered how I could possibly endure this for the long journey. A direct entry from my journal: "I move slow and steady, yet I feel like a waterfall."

A four-door, manual transmission grey Clio awaited my arrival at Charles de Gaulle airport. My energy was waning due to the lengthy air travel, yet I mustered up enough strength to hit the highway. Thomas' brother, Christophe, his wife Dawn, children Thomas and Morgane, had rented a home in Brittany. A four hour drive loomed ahead. Finding myself grateful that my vehicle had a wonderful sound system I took in the lovely scenery. Fall colors of crimson and gold exploded in all directions.

As I arrived at my destination, exhaustion kicked in.

"I can't meet you for dinner with Bernard." I messaged Dawn via WhatsApp.

We agreed to connect in the morning, the day of Thomas' memorial service.

I awoke to a robotic lawnmower diligently working outside. Birds chirped. Church bells rang. An aroma of smoke filled the air. Wind rustled through the trees. The magic of Brittany's countryside was on full display.

A Love Letter to Thomas

Thomas' extended family had always welcomed me with open arms. Today would prove to be no exception. Arriving at Bernard's home in La Poterie, I felt a heaviness. It would be the first in-person encounter with him after Thomas' death. Aromas of cooked meat, stale air, and urine filled the space. Bernard sat in his usual chair facing the television, surrounded by old newspapers, photos of Thomas and his deceased wife, and the ever-present bottle of whisky by his side. Making my way over to him, I asked for Spirit's guidance to remain peaceful.

"Bonjour Eve." Bernard said weakly. Tears filled his eyes.

"Bonjour" I kissed him on both cheeks.

"My wife is dead. My son is dead." Despair was painted on his face.

"I know. My husband is dead. But we are still here!" I exclaimed.

Christophe and Dawn began speaking to Bernard in French. Again, my limited ability to comprehend the dialogue served me well. Voices continued to increase in volume and intensity.

"He says he's not going to the service." Dawn shared with me.

"Yeah, he is embarrassed to be seen." Christophe added.

Frustration bubbled inside of me. Not thinking clearly, perhaps due to the jet lag, I positioned myself directly in front of Bernard, hands on my hips.

"Bernard. I did not travel over 5,000 miles for you to

not attend the ceremony! You need to get up out of your chair, clean up, and get over there! I insist!" My nostrils flared.

He pouted his lips. Dawn, a nurse, took on the charge of cleaning him up. She and Christophe made plans to get Bernard to the service, taking place by the lake in La Poterie.

One hurdle jumped. Whew!

Lunch was planned for forty guests at the family home, a converted church (St. Yves) situated lakeside. This is where Thomas grew up, frolicking in the forests, sowing his wild oats, and connecting with nature. Cousin Boris grilled St. Jacques (scallops) and bacon on an open fire to serve as an aperitif (appetizer). Following Spirit's lead, I assisted with setting rectangular tables inside, end to end, placing freshly laundered white tablecloths atop the wooden surface. Wine decanters overflowing with flowers provided a splash of color and warmth.

Wine and champagne flowed freely. Christophe sat at the head of the table.

"Time to eat!" someone shouted.

When all were seated, Christophe raised his glass of wine.

"To Thomas!" he exclaimed.

"To Thomas!" the group cried out.

Glancing around the room, I felt Spirit's presence. An abundance of love was evident. Looking down at my place setting, I noticed a plastic skull. It was the only one on the table. With the Gaelic festival of Samhain approaching, celebrated widely in Celtic countries, I found this to be a sign from Thomas, reminding me that death is inevitable.

Culinary delights appeared out of nowhere. Homemade quiche, mushroom chili, and rice were served family style. My taste buds danced with delight. Conversation was lively. People enjoyed connecting and sharing stories.

Close to the end of the meal, I asked Christophe to help translate my words into French. Standing to address the group, I grabbed the heavy bag lying at my feet.

"I know how special Thomas was to every single one of you. As a reminder of that, I brought a unique glass heart for each of you, which includes a small amount of Thomas' ashes."

There were gasps. A few people cried. Some had shocked looks on their faces. I knew this gesture was out of the ordinary, most likely a first for everyone there. Christophe informed everyone I that had carried these in my luggage all the way from California. For most of these people, not having a body to bury was an unfortunate reality. However, now that they had a "piece" of Thomas, they could be at ease. Cousin Tiphane took me aside.

"Eve. This is beautiful. I'm so happy." A tear slowly rolled down her right cheek.

We all took to cleaning up the space, returning tables and chairs back to their original locations, washing dishes, then transitioning to the formal gathering.

An announcement sharing our event had been published in the local paper. Close to 330 people were expected to attend! Uncle Ivan spent several months building a wooden terrace, jutting out over the lake, holding up to 100 people. I went with the flow. People arrived slowly. Bernard sat in a folding chair next to the car he arrived in. People offered condolences. My stoicism remained intact until the gates of grief were flung open. My journal entry recalls the interaction:

"I held it together until Rico appeared. Tears were flowing. I knew it would be hardest when the friends arrived: Francois, Carol, David, and Thomas. My desire was to hug all of them, yet the French don't do that. It sucks. I'm very touch-focused, particularly when consoling people."

A tree in Thomas' honor was to be planted nearby. After a short program, we gathered around the burial site. Again, a direct excerpt from my journal:

"Christophe and I dumped ashes into the hole. People clapped and there was a sign of relief. Closure. Cousin Marion sat at the base of the tree and played a Tibetan brass singing bowl. Some people put their glass heart in the hole. My judgment about throwing money away had to be dismissed. There was an abundance of joy, combined with sadness. I could only imagine how difficult this had been for the family and friends. Not knowing their traditions, it's hard for me to comprehend their experience. Rain, gentle drops, began to fall. Items were picked up, shade structure dismantled. A double-rainbow appeared – another sign?"

A Love Letter to Thomas

_____

Aside from aiding in closure for Thomas' family and friends, there was business to complete during my short stay. As fortune would have it, I inherited the home that Thomas owned, and Bernard was now living in. Spirit led me to let go of this property, returning it to the family, as I had neither attachment to it, nor the desire to manage ownership from afar.

"It's rare that a person denounces their inheritance." Yann, the notaire (notary), stated in a curious tone.

Christophe, Uncle Serge, and I were gathered in the living room of the family's lakeside home. Yann's lack of response to my emails over the previous months did not provide me with any reassurance that this would go smoothly. However, I trusted Christophe to translate on my behalf and bring clarity to the situation. Yann unpacked his mobile office consisting of a keyboard, mouse, portable WiFi, and a large monitor.

Proceedings began. Multiple documents were displayed one after another on the monitor. Yann spoke no English and rarely looked at me. I retained my power with a strong stance and attentiveness.

"First, you will give Yann power of attorney." Christophe instructed me.

"Where are the physical documents?" I was suspicious. Uneasiness came over me.

"You will receive them after you sign."

In my experience, this was highly irregular. We don't do this in the United States. However, I continued to trust

147

the process and moved forward as advised. It was seamless. Documents signed, files closed, emails sent. Completion.

There was commotion outside. Turning my head in the direction of a paned, window-topped Dutch door, I saw rain. Not just drops, buckets. A torrential downpour. I equated that atmospheric episode to Thomas shedding tears for the transaction, particularly the part about me keeping my word not to evict Bernard from his home.

Our next task was to finalize the paperwork with Bernard. An entry from my journal:

"The rain stopped when we needed to go see Bernard. I'm sure it must be a challenge for him, to be in a body that doesn't work properly. He refuses to wear diapers and continues to soil himself and his bed. The aroma is overwhelming. How can he stand to live in those conditions? The notaire introduced himself and explained the process. Bernard signed a power of attorney as well, with the house being transferred to Christophe soon. I'm delighted that the kids (Morgane and Thomas) will have a place to stay when they visit Brittany. And it's very close to the forest where Thomas and I went mushroom foraging with his mom. I can recall the aromas, musty air, cool temperature, shape of knife, and basket. One of our first outings together. Uncle Serge and the notaire left. Christophe and Bernard argued. The tone of their voices was abrasive. Leaning into the Science of Mind philosophy, I remained in a state of compassion and understanding."

A Love Letter to Thomas

Before departing, I leaned over to Bernard, cupping his face with both of my hands.

"Be nice." I whispered.

Bernard smiled.

"Be nice."

He winked.

Cousin Cedric owned a sailboat, docked in Port Dahouet. The following day, he invited our small group (Christophe, Dawn, Morgane, Thomas and myself) out for a short tour. Giddy with excitement, I climbed aboard.

"Let me give you a tour." Cedric insisted

Comfortably sparse, I imagined how romantic it was for him and his wife to have a break from children, sailing on the open sea with salty air spraying their faces, sleeping under a blanket of stars at night. Serenity personified.

"I brought a handful of Thomas' ashes. Let's dump them out at some point."

Morgane and Thomas bowed their heads. I felt their grief. It was a continual struggle for them, the processing of letting go.

"How about here?" Cedric stated.

I looked to the sky. "Perfect!"

Wind at our backs, I pulled the plastic bag from my

jacket pocket.

"Morgane, Thomas. Hold the bag with me." They acquiesced.

My fingers held the opening revealing the grey, sandy ashes. Particles of bone could be seen. The three of us held a side, turning the bag upside down. Contents were released into the wind, carrying them into the English Channel. A gorgeous, turquoise color with hints of cerulean blue, sparkling in the sunlight. Another completion.

A Love Letter to Thomas

"*Wouldn't it be wonderful if a group of individuals arrived on Earth who were for something and not against something.*"
— *Ernest Holmes*

The Elephant in the Room

By now, I'm almost certain a question has been weighing on my reader's mind. What happened to the driver of the car that hit Thomas? This is where the rubber truly meets the road, spiritually speaking.

As I shared earlier, a young man and I had locked eyes over Thomas' unconscious body lying listless on the pavement. To me, he was just a bystander. In reality, he was the driver. Reasonably surreal, don't you think?

The police report included evidence of THC and THC metabolite in the blood sample as well as proof of handling two cell phones simultaneously. A direct message received via Instagram on one of them at 7:11:45 PM said, "Yeo, what size pants do you rock!? I make custom and was thinking that I wanna send you a pair! LMK." The police report identified 7:12 PM as the time of impact.

Before the evidence was revealed to me, I had come to a place of peace with the circumstances. Accidents happen. The driver could have sneezed, causing him to turn the steering wheel as a result. Several friends adamantly concluded intoxication was the cause. Judgments were rampant. This frustrated me immensely.

My training as a Prayer Practitioner kicked into high gear. It was imperative that I continued to stay aligned with Spirit, with unassailable certainty that the outcome was an aspect of the Divine Plan. After all, many of us are guilty of distracted driving, right? There, but for the grace of God, go I.

After the police investigation was completed, I was advised that a Prosecutor from the Summit County

District Attorney's office, Trish Cassell, would be contacting me. Formal charges were being drafted, and a hearing was scheduled for June 8th, 123 days after the accident. Due to the pandemic, all court appearances would occur via Zoom. Multiple conversations via email and conference calls between both sides focused on a quick resolution. I agreed.

On August 10th, the driver pled guilty to a Class A misdemeanor. He would serve 120 days in jail, participate in substance abuse counseling, and write me a letter of apology. He began his sentence on August 17th with an expected release date of December 17th. On November 5th, I received the following email from DA Trish Cassell:

> "Just today, I learned that Watson [not his real name] was released yesterday. The jail gave him 40 days 'good time.' This is time, calculated by the jail, that we have no control over. If someone is 'good' and doesn't cause problems, the jail gives them credit for that."

Now, knowing this, how should I proceed? My intention was to send Watson a book, *Dark Nights of the Soul* by Thomas Moore. Now it was too late to do so, at least to the jail address.

This book had been gifted to me on April 25, 2020 by Hugh Foster. I read it over the course of seven weeks, underlining passages and creating marginalia.

Dark Nights of the Soul is a challenging read, in that the subject matter prompts readers to dive deep into aspects of their life which are difficult to face. There is a plethora of videos online interviewing people in similar circumstances who wallow in the muck of their consequences daily. This was a book that would, in my mind, serve Watson well in the long run. Despite his sentence being abbreviated and, for some, not severe enough, I knew he would be living in his own private prison for the remainder of his life.

My heart ached for Watson. Continuous prayer requests were submitted for Peace. I felt compelled to forgive him out loud, in person. Perhaps that would transpire in the not-too-distant future.

A Love Letter to Thomas

"It does not matter what you bear,
but how you bear it."
— Seneca

Trials and Tribulations

Celebration of Life complete. Criminal case in process. Pandemic ever-present. What next? Something within me felt compelled to move forward with a civil case. After all, this was a hit-and-run accident where the driver was on the clock with his employer, a local ski rental delivery company with multiple locations serving resorts throughout the United States. This was a serious matter. The company was liable and needed to be held accountable. I called up my friend Lisa Sutton.

"Hey, Lisa. It's Eve. I need your advice."

Lisa had been another angel of mine throughout the days after Thomas' death. Despite being entrenched with managing her deceased mother's complicated estate, she compiled a packet of valuable information for me with: resources on grief, checklists of tasks to complete, and entities to contact for cancelling a myriad of accounts. She also held an arsenal of legal advice based on the nature of Thomas' accident.

"Oh, Eve. You know I would do anything for you." Lisa said plainly.

"I am thinking of proceeding with a civil case. Do you know any attorneys?"

Lisa and her partner Dave had property in Park City. They were very connected to the community. I was certain they could help.

"Yes! You can talk with Dennis Ferguson, Dave's buddy from college. He is not a criminal attorney, yet he would be a great person to have on your team."

A Love Letter to Thomas

We arranged to call Dennis together. A follow-up email from him stated the following:

> Hi, Eve. My first choice would be Colin King. He is a Fellow of The American College of Trial Lawyers, very experienced and respected. I talked to him about your case and can assure you that you would get the best personal attention. I will send you his contact information but will also be happy to introduce you if you're interested.

I immediately reached out to Colin. We talked at length, planning the next steps. Right from the start, we set the intention for our case to NOT go to trial. This point is important for my reader to comprehend. Having been exposed to friends and families who had participated in civil trials, my desire was to eliminate this from my experience. Particularly with the pandemic, both Colin and I knew that a trial could be pushed off for years. If this were to happen, evidence may be lost, witness' memories could fade, and momentum would slow down.

Over the course of seven months, the team at Dewsnup King Olsen Woral Havas began building a case in preparation for going to trial. This was a typical methodology. Thoroughness was necessary. A mechanical engineer worked on gathering details from law enforcement agencies to reconstruct the accident. Economic experts requested my financial information related to the business, using it to calculate economic loss and damages to request. Throughout the process, I continued to rely on affirmative prayer, treating that we would settle this case without going to trial.

In early October, I received a call from my attorney.

Exit

Eve Chauvel

"Eve, I have great news!" Colin said excitedly.

"Great to hear from you. What is it?"

"The ski rental company wants to mediate the case!"

I was elated. Colin explained further:

"This is a first step in the right direction. However, some mediations can go on for days and never reach an agreement. Be prepared for that to occur."

My learning curve continued to expand. Again, I trusted that my team excelled at their respective jobs, and everything would unfold just as it should. The mediation was scheduled for October 26th in Denver, Colorado, where the defendant's attorney's offices were located. I was grateful we were not going to Utah. It was too soon for me to even consider going back to the state where Thomas died. Flights booked, hotel room arranged for, mental preparations began.

On the morning of October 25th, my daughter's 27th birthday, the weather report showed Denver was anticipating unexpected snowfall. Damn. What would happen now? I reflected on a quote from Mara Pennell, "Don't resist what is coming right in front of us. There is always a higher idea." Again, Spirit had different plans for me. Upon arrival at John Wayne Airport, I discovered my fight was cancelled! No alerts were sent to my phone, as is typical. My emotions took over me. Tears streaming down my face, I attempted to compose myself with the ticket agent.

"It is critical I get to Denver today." I implored.

"There is a flight departing at 6:30 PM from LAX.

158

A Love Letter to Thomas

You've automatically been booked on it."

"That's a ridiculous option." My nerves were on edge now. If I took this flight, I wouldn't arrive until 10:00 p.m.

The agent continued to look for other possibilities.

"You could purchase a new ticket on a different airline."

I played out the scenarios in my head. Getting to Denver tonight was imperative. The best option was to book a fight on Southwest, departing at 4:30 pm. and arriving much later than the originally scheduled 5:00 PM What do to with the time? My desire was to hang out in the airport bar, drink a Bloody Mary or two. I opted to go home. This was the more conscious decision. I realized my emotions were still raw, and the comfort of home would serve my greatest good, providing grounding.

On returning home via Uber, the first thing I did was to light a stick of incense. Nag Champa, to be exact. Patchouli and sandalwood aromas filled the room, gifting me with a peaceful tranquility that the airport environment would not have provided. Home. Safety. Security. Ninety minutes to fill, I spent it emptying the dishwasher, sipping green tea, and reading. An unusual circumstance arose. One of the light switches in my bedroom hadn't been working properly for quite some time. This morning, it became functional again for a short period of time. Right before my Uber arrived, I tried the switch again. It worked! I took this as a sign of approval for deciding to come home instead of morphing into a bar fly, which would not have served my highest good. Feeling more centered, I returned to the airport. While waiting to board, the song "Higher Love" by Steve Winwood began playing. Another reminder from the Universe, at least from my perspective.

Arrival at the Denver airport was met with trepidation. I don't like the cold. The temperature was frigid. The last time I saw the snow fall was in Park City, Utah during my anniversary ski trip. Another coincidence? An Uber driver transported me to my hotel, the Sheraton Denver Downtown. Colin was expecting my call.

"Hey, Eve. You finally got in!" Colin spoke in an excited tone.

"Yes. What a day! I could use a drink."

"I've already started."

We agreed to meet in the bar fifteen minutes later.

My room was pleasant, minimally furnished, with a King-sized bed. My body collapsed requiring a few minutes of rest before my meeting. I recalled that when Thomas and I moved into our home, our bed was Queen-sized so that the space could be maximized. We quickly determined that a King bed would be better suited for his 6-foot frame, not to mention our sexual escapades which required ample mattress real estate. It is reported that humans spend approximately one-third of their life sleeping. Why not make it the most comfortable experience possible?

Snapping myself back to the present moment, I pushed myself upright, collected my purse, and exited the room.

Colin was waiting for me at a low table with four swivel chairs.

"Well, hello there, beautiful lady." Colin rose up out of his chair.

We hugged. This was our second time meeting in person. The first was when he was in Orange County for a deposition.

Dinner was ordered, drinks were delivered, and we discussed the plan for the next day.

"We are scheduled to begin at 9:00 AM so let's meet for breakfast at 8:00 a.m."

I agreed. That would give me plenty of time to continue with my morning spiritual practice of meditation and the Science of Mind Magazine Daily Guide entry. Our conversation was cordial, both of us exchanging personal stories, sharing respective journeys which led us to this current place in time. One last drink, whisky neat, was the punctuation mark at the end of our night.

Sleep came easily to me. The snow continued to fall. I was grateful to be inside, protected from the elements. Not like the houseless population; they were always on my mind when the weather turned cold. When I was a child, I thought it would be fun to run away and live on the street. Now, as an adult, I recognize that was a ridiculous idea, not glamorous as I once thought.

My 6:30 AM alarm jarred me awake. Here we go. Spirit is on my side. Naturally, I was a tad anxious. How would this unfold? I continued to trust the process, knowing that Colin and his team had done all they could to present evidence which would clearly indicate a win for our side if this case went to trial. I sent an intention for the mediation to end by noon.

Breakfast was brief. I felt confident that the day would unfold perfectly, I would catch my regularly scheduled flight back to Orange County, and this aspect of our case would be closed. Exiting the hotel, Colin and I walked in the freshly fallen snow for five minutes to a nearby office building. My breathing practice kicked in. This was one of my saving graces throughout the trials and tribulations of life. For me, it connects me more deeply to Source. I wonder if people who smoke have the same sensation. After all, they are inhaling and exhaling rather deeply on a very regular basis, right?

The elevator took us up to our designated floor. We checked in with the receptionist, who led us into our conference room, a typical space with moderately-glossed oak table and eight, black-leather swivel chairs.   .

"Eve, Colin, this is Joe. He will be mediating your case today."

For those not familiar with how mediation unfolds, here is the gist of the process. Mediation is a negotiation facilitated by a third party. Both sides sit in separate rooms, never seeing each other face-to-face. The mediator talks with each side, asking questions, gathering information, and presenting offers as needed. Settling on agreed damages is the goal, yet this doesn't always happen. I was forewarned that we could extend the mediation, if an agreement wasn't reached by the end of the day.

Joe, impeccably dressed in a well-fitted suit, extended his hand.

"Nice to meet you. My condolences for your loss."

"Thank you."

We congregated around a long, shiny conference table. My armpits began to sweat. Breathing exercises kicked in. A range of emotions were moving through my consciousness. I continued to trust the process, letting Spirit guide our way. For the first time, I was shown arial view of the crime scene. Unprepared for this, I quickly became tearful. Flashbacks of the event came fast. My breathing quickened. Hands shook. Returning to my spiritual practice, I repeated Science of Mind principles in my mind: Love, Light, Life, Peace, Beauty, Joy and Truth.

Ultimately, we finished the mediation before noon and settled on a number that was higher than Colin's team had specified as their goal. Joe spoke:

> "In my entire career of mediating over 4,000 cases I have never participated in such a smooth and rapid mediation."

For me, this was another demonstration of the power our mind has. Clearly state your intention, visualize what you desire, let go, see what happens, allowing Spirit to do the work, here and now.

Then, I requested to meet the team who represented the ski rental company's insurance firm. The room fell silent. My intention was to thank them for their contribution to our process and give them each a 'Be Nice' bag. The look of shock on their faces spoke volumes. The negotiator invited them into our room, and one by one I shook each 'opponent's' hand, presenting each with a bag. Smiles all around; it was a divinely ordained completion.

Colin and I celebrated at a restaurant in town called Rioja, on Larimer Street in the LODO area of Denver. Due to the weather, we opted to travel via the light rail system. I always enjoy traveling by local transportation as it provides a window on the world with a lovely view. In

Thomas' honor, we ordered a bottle of Champagne and French Dip sandwiches. Truly a comfort meal. On the way out, I noticed bottles of Juan Gil Sauvignon Blanc on the wall. If you recall, this was the white wine we purchased at Trader Joe's on a regular basis to have on hand. While walking out the door, the song "Calling All Angels" by Train started playing on the restaurant's radio. I also found $40 hidden in my purse.

I was ready to go home. This heavy burden that had been carried on my shoulders for months was complete. My journal entry from the day ended with one simple sentence:

"On the flight back to O.C., I am amazed at the almost full moon in a dark sky illuminating all that is below in its wake."

A Love Letter to Thomas

"The spiritual journey involves going beyond hope and fear,
stepping into the unknown territory,
continually moving forward.
The most important aspect of being
on the spiritual path may be to just keep moving."
— Pema Chodron

Coping and Blessings in Disguise

The question I've been asked time and time again is, "How did you do it?" The "it" most people are referring to is coping with the sudden, tragic loss of my husband, coupled with our business being completely shut down due to the pandemic. The short answer? One word. Faith. The long answer? It takes a village with an arsenal of tools at the ready.

Again, there are no coincidences, unless Einstein was right when he said, "Coincidence is God's way of remaining anonymous." I had implicit trust that Spirit would provide me with what I needed to stay sane, grounded, and able to surmount my grief.

With restrictions in place in terms of travel and engaging in normal activities, an activity I turned to was books. I've always enjoyed literature on various topics. Mystery, romance, realistic fiction, self-help, biographies, most everything appealed to me. One of my dearest friends, Teri Broughton, gifted me with *The Hot Young Widows Club* which was quite humorous (much needed). The author, Nora McInerny, delves into the depths of what it's like to experience loss, giving readers valuable insight into the grieving process and how to support those who are grieving. Additionally, she founded an actual club which I joined, immediately buying a t-shirt with the club's name on it. I wore it only once, concluding that I didn't want my identity to be that of a widow. In fact, I changed the relationship status on my Facebook profile from Married, to Widowed, to Single in quick succession after Thomas' passing.

I must say, my favorite topic of Nora's book

addressed moving on with a new relationship. That hit home for me. A mere two months after Thomas' death, I began developing feelings for another man. Nora's words validated my desire to continue down this new romantic path. I granted myself permission to do so.

Another book that helped me immensely was *Finding Meaning: The Sixth Stage of Grief* by David Kessler. I devoured the electronic version. During my Prayer Practitioner education, we covered death and dying at length. A required text was *On Grief and Grieving: Finding the Meaning of Grief Through the Five Stages of Loss*, which he co-authored with Elizabeth Kübler-Ross. Due to the pandemic, David was unable to travel the world on a book tour promoting the release of his new text. He resorted to holding regular live discussions on Facebook which I tuned into with regularity. Here is what most hit home for me:

- Secondary grief is real. This is when friends and/or family do not show up for us in the way we desire. It's always about them and not us.

- Grief is on the inside; bereavement is on the outside.

The overarching coping mechanism was composed of my spiritual practices. I continued meditating, attending services at O.C. Spiritual Center, reading the Daily Guide in *Science of Mind Magazine*, and using affirmative prayer. I returned to journaling, albeit thirty-three days after Thomas' death. My first entry was written on March 10th during Rev. Janet Moore's Tuesday night class:

"Finally putting pen to paper after I became a widow at 8:00 PM on February 6, 2020. One day after my four-year wedding anniversary. THIS SUCKS!

Janet's Class: Share about your vision for a better world and how you are creating it in your life.

Having people plant trees in Thomas' name, 120 to date.

• Talk less, listen more.

• Manifestations

• Actively and consciously co-create life.

• We never know what effect — even just one word — has on others.

I must cling to the knowing that there is a spiritual perfection in all people, regardless of appearances. Eve, you can do this because of your strong faith and high level of consciousness. Baby steps. What can I learn from these experiences? Not bad but limited. Thought is key. Look at what I *get* to do. Treat every action with loving kindness. Be mindful of how I am functioning so that any forthcoming good isn't cut off. PAY ATTENTION TO MIRACLES (even the little tiny ones)! I'm so glad I came to class tonight. So many reminders and reinforcing activities that I'm on the right path. Thomas is at peace as an eternal being. It's just that he was able to go to the next experience before me. Science of

Mind teaches us how to live THIS life! My healing journey is always perfect. Make certain I don't take things personally. Know the perfect, divine pattern. An absence of (fill in the blank) leads to unconscious choices and unproductive lives. Just breathe. Let go. Increase my treatments. More frequent use of the tools because they work! Always come from a place of finding a better idea."

Journaling was a wondrous outlet to release my thoughts in a safe space. Now, as I'm writing this book, having these source materials at the ready was necessary to refresh my memory.

Fortunately, my spiritual community rallied around me, providing regular contact through all possible means. Several lifelines were available to me. I placed multiple late-night calls to other Practitioners. One of which was to Anne Perrah, a dear soul who had traveled with our group to Ireland. She and her husband, John, had relocated to Reno, Nevada a few years ago. She answered immediately.

"Anne, I am having a tough time sleeping."

"Oh, dear one. I understand," Anne uttered softly

"The images of the accident keep appearing in my head. It's very disturbing."

She continued consoling me, suggesting that I use a form of grief yoga to help me self-soothe during trying times. I was to lay on the bed, curl up in a ball, pull my knees into my chest, and wrap my arms around my shins. This type of hugging myself tightly is like the position we assume while in utero. It's incredibly comforting. I encourage you to try it, regardless of whether or not you believe that you need it. It's free and doesn't hurt. Trust me. The benefits are real.

I also welcomed the opportunity to join two different grief groups. One was in person and another online. The in-person group was held at a local church, incredibly heavy in tone, and was not a good fit for me. It was not aligned with my belief system at all, so I opted to leave after only one session. The online group was conducted via Zoom by Vivian Clecak. She is a dear friend whom I've known for twenty years. Vivian, along with two other women, founded Human Options, a non-profit in Irvine, California whose mission is to break the cycle of family violence. I served on their board for twelve years. Her grief group met via Zoom for several weeks. Assignments were given which included aspects of exploring grief. We learned how to break out of the stereotypes about the period of grief, bringing words of connection and understanding to the group. Our "business of dying" was underway. Some of the key aspects of our sharing included answering the following questions:

- What role(s) did my partner play in my life?

- How did my partner round me out?

- What do I want right now?

- What early grief have I already overcome?

- What moments were most difficult?

- What moments were most helpful?

- How can I discharge my rage in appropriate ways?

A Love Letter to Thomas

- How can I be more responsible for my own self-care?

- How can I live a life that will honor my loved one?

Fundamentally, the experience brought me to a new awareness that grief and gratitude can co-exist. In fact, it's critical that I embrace this knowing because none of us get out of this world alive:

Grief will be a part of life.
It is the duty of the living to live!
I am able to transform pain into joy.

Eve Chauvel

A Love Letter to Thomas

---

*"Spirit is only available in the here and now
and is unlimited in what it can reveal
as to the depth of your existence."*
— Dr. Jim Turrell

Visions, Dreams and Healing

My fascination with the afterlife, what comes next, has been a constant in my life. Curiosity can get the best of me at times. Spiritual signs are abundant. We can see them if we let go and allow them to come forward. Since Thomas' death, I have had more experiences with the spiritual realm in a shorter period of time than ever before. Three of which I will share here.

On April 5th, two months after Thomas died, I had an experience that reminded me of my connection to Source via a dream. My journal entry from that day states the following:

> After a bath last night, I reached out to my friend Julie (heartsdesirecounsel.com) for a reading. We both set the intention for Thomas to come into my dreams. He did! I had gotten up to use the bathroom then come back to bed. He arrived when I fell back asleep, and we were spooning. He squeezed me so very hard and tight. It felt so good. I asked him what it's like to be where he is. He pointed to the sky then drew the word "YEAR" with his finger in the sky. When I turned to look at his face, telling him that the accident was so bad and beginning to cry, he disappeared.

This was implausible to me. There was not one indication regarding what the word 'year' indicated. Could it have been a premonition? At that time, the pandemic was progressing with no clarity regarding its potential end. However, hindsight is twenty-twenty, right?

A Love Letter to Thomas

- The pandemic lockdown lasted one year.

- OC Spiritual Center's Easter service was held one year later, where I was one of several orators during the program.

The second point is important to share, because my spiritual community has been vital in my healing process. They have been a solid foundation for me throughout the ten years I've been a member. Without their undying love, caring, and support, I know I wouldn't be the person I am today. These are people who embrace the Science of Mind philosophy and teachings, implementing an abundance of unconditional love to all. I am blessed. I am grateful.

I continued to ask Spirit for more time with Thomas in my dreams. Nine months after his passing, I was granted another opportunity. This is a direct entry from my journal, dated November 6, 2020:

"I woke up around 4:00 AM tossed and turned for a bit then back to sleep. My sense is I was between waking and sleeping when I felt someone pulling back the sheet to climb into bed with me. At first, I thought it was the man I was dating which startled me. 'How did you get in my house?' His face was not clear, so I touched it and there was no facial hair. Right then I knew it was Thomas. He climbed on top of me, and I hugged him. I heard mechanical noises almost as if Thomas was a robot. There was a bright light surrounding us alternating between blue and white. It flashed occasionally. I thanked Thomas for coming and took the experience in, completely wanting to use as many senses as possible. I can't recall aromas or tastes. Thomas mumbled something incoherent. Gradually his body relaxed and melted away with the colors becoming a blanket of stars. I was overjoyed, not sad at all. Daylight was breaking so I wondered what time it was. I looked at my phone – 5:55 a.m.

The final experience I will share was very short, yet revelatory.

Moving through grief seemed insurmountable at times. Despite my training as a prayer practitioner, the big question – why did this happen – loomed. One night, I received a bit of insight. Again in a dream, Thomas appeared. His smiling face greeted me, his warm and tender hand reached out, caressing my face. "My love" he said "I had to go so you could do something greater."

That was it. He vanished. No specifics about what the "greater something" was. To this day, I continue to explore what that indicated. A few ideas have crossed my mind, yet does it really matter? Do I need a definitive answer? Perhaps the only thing greater is me living my life NOW, in the moment. Anything other than death can be considered greater, don't you think? Therein lies the crux, thinking. Perhaps thinking needs to go by the wayside and I need to focus more on feeling. All the feels.

A Love Letter to Thomas

"*Be in a state of gratitude for everything
that shows up in your life.
Be thankful for the storms
as well as the smooth sailing.*"
— Dr. Wayne Dyer

Epilogue

Writing this book was an uphill battle, on a scale of one to ten, it was an average of eight. It began with an idea then moved into quick action. A majority of the writing was done in a very short period of a few months. I would like to tell you that my method was structured, planned out, and intentional. It was nothing of the sort. Some days the writing flowed, other days it was nonexistent. I recall Dr. Jim Turrell saying there is no such thing as writer's block. Writers write. What they write may be gibberish or incoherent, but they write, either for a designated period or, perhaps, a certain number of words per day. Not me. I simply wrote when inspired to do so.

However, I did capture my thoughts by using presentation-sized sticky paper, one for each category of subject matter: Early Years, The Accident, The Pandemic, Grief, and General Notes. Then, using colored 2" x 2" sticky notes, one color for each subject, I wrote topics as they came to me, placing them in the associated subject. This worked well as I could move the notes around to make more logical sense as the writing continued. Going with the flow was a natural feeling for my first stab at being a writer. From the start, my goal was to write at least as many words as were in "Tuesdays With Morrie" by Mitch Albom. One source stated that his book contained 35,000 words. That seemed achievable. My final word count is 40,735. Mission accomplished!

Naturally, a range of emotions rose inside. Memories returned with zeal. They were mostly pleasant with the occasional knockdown, drag out internal wrestling match, sometimes a waterfall of tears winning out. Swollen, blood shot eyes seemed to be a normal feature of my outward appearance.

What kept me going? Why did I persist with this seeming nonsense? I did this primarily to leave a legacy about Thomas, but also for you. This story needed to be written for your edification. I feel that the Universe has been giving me material to write about for decades. For now, this story is the one I *had* to write. It could very well be the first of many. Only time will tell. But knowing what I know now, the Science of Mind philosophy has been my guiding light in this journey, for which I am grateful.

Tomorrow is promised to no one, so please, I beg of you, make peace with your past, forgive yourself along with others, and stay true to who you are. This world needs your authentic self to shine. Shine brightly.

Mark Twain is quoted as saying, "The two most important days in your life are the day you are born and the day you find out why." What's your why? Whatever it is, go and do it. Now. Don't hesitate. Live this one beautiful life you have now and do it with gratitude for all the moments.

Eve Chauvel

A Final Letter to Thomas

A Love Letter to Thomas

Dear MBL (My Breton Lover),

Three years have passed since you transitioned. By the time this book is published, it will be almost three and a half — approximately 1,840,822 minutes. I know, it's a strange measurement, but you know how I like numbers and analysis.

This book has been a labor of love, cathartic and healing. Thank you is all I have in the moment. As I continue to share with others, I feel as if the Universe has been giving me a story to write about, all of my life. Here it is. It's a gift to help others heal and know the spiritual truths which apply to everyone, regardless. Of course, you knew this was your path, didn't you? A spiritual vehicle to help others know these truths, even though you didn't believe the Science of Mind Philosophy was real.

I love you so much... so much that all I can continue saying is thank you. Thank you for helping me believe in true, unconditional love. You allowed me the freedom to be who I am within the confines of a marital commitment, filled with trust, honesty, lots of love... and sex too!

There is so much life ahead of me — and I'm excited! I read a book about living until you're 120 and I thought, why not 130? So, that is my goal. (I claimed this in my journal.)

I hope the adventure of flying around the Universe is as much fun as you expected it to be. I wonder: was that you riding on the Neowise Comet when I was in Joshua Tree for a photo shoot in 2020?

Au Revior, Thomas
See you soon!
YBE (Your Beautiful Eve)

A Love Letter to Thomas

A Letter of Apology
from Watson
[Pseudonym]

April 8, 2020

Dear Ms. Chauvel,

This letter has been weighing so heavily on my heart and my mind. I wanted to reach out and let you know how terrible and completely distraught and sorrowful I have felt since the tragic accident occurred in Park City on the evening of February 6th.

I cannot even imagine the feelings that you and your family must feel. It has torn at me every moment since I stopped the van and saw and realized what had happened. Please know that I never saw Mr. Chauvel in the street and I have replayed that moment through my mind a thousand times and the answer stays the same, "I never saw him to avoid him." It has awakened me almost every night while I try to sleep. It is the worst feeling and the worst situation I have ever experienced in my life. I am so sorry for your loss and I just want you to know that my heart breaks for you and your family, it is such a scary accident, but it happened somehow, and I cannot understand why?

I am not a reckless young man; I value and respect the life and humanity of all the people and friends and family around me. To that point, I am not sure if writing you will help you feel any better or take away any pain and suffering. However, if I can do anything in my power to say I am sorry and apologize then that is a place I want to start from.

Never in my young life, did I ever envision a tragedy like this taking place. I've driven the ski rental van through Park City and the surrounding area now for the past couple of ski seasons, and now I will not do that anymore because I am terrified and scared of driving on the dark roads.

I was so scared and in shock, I couldn't think calmly or rationally and when the police showed up the officer told people to get away, I reacted very juvenile and drove the van away so I could call my girlfriend and tell her I loved her and that a terrible accident had happened. I have my own issues with blood and trauma due to autoimmune disease called Steven Johnson Syndrome that almost took my life back in high school. It's something that I wouldn't want anyone to endure and It has personally left me scarred, emotionally immature, and unstable when it comes to trauma and injury, which I contribute to my juvenile behavior.

After composing myself, I returned to the scene and knew that not only was a man's life possibly taken without any intent or malice, but his entire family was traumatized and broken. This is the reality: that I cannot understand why it happened and I have been praying to God for his forgiveness, wisdom and some level of strength to get through all of this tragedy.

To me, even more importantly, I want to confess to you my sorrow and terrible sadness and let you know that I truly never saw Mr. Chauvel to try and stop or avoid him that night. There are no real words I can offer that make this any better or easier. It is the most terrible thing I have ever had to try and understand and so far, I am still unable to have it make sense.

When I was sitting in the jail that night, I just wept myself to sleep until they let me make a phone call at about 2am, and I called my dad who lives in California. He asked me what happened and all I could say is that it was dark and I didn't see anyone in the street and I hit a pedestrian and he died. He helped get me out of jail that night. It's a place I never thought I would be in and it's a place I never want to visit or be taken to again. It forced a young man to age 10 years overnight and as of today, I just work at hanging onto my thoughts. I have been seeing a doctor to help me handle the severe trauma and stress and hope and pray that you and your family will find it in your heart to forgive me and to know that this was an accident.

I could not wish a worse scenario for you and your family. For me it has been a terrible nightmare that wakes me up most every night in panic. I am so sorry and I want you to know that I have been praying every night that you and God will find the grace to forgive me and to make some sense of this because I have been struggling to do the same. I am praying for your family to heal and get through this tragedy.

My life is never going to be the same or as simple and carefree as it was, and I will carry this with me for my entire life, as will you and your family. I am completely torn up and just wish there was something I could do to change that night. In the end, it is up to God now and I hope he is kind and gracious to you and your family.

My heart goes out to you and my own heart is hurting badly, I offer this with all my tears and sorrow and with every ounce of respect in my body and soul.

Watson

A Love Letter to Thomas

Eve Chauvel

Acknowledgements

A nearly insurmountable task looms before me - to properly acknowledge the hundreds of people who empowered me to write this book. Without exception, everyone who was mentioned by name in the content is honored in perpetuity – you're in a book! Many people relish the mere thought of this possibility. However, allow me this space to call out the following groups and people, in no order of importance.

Dr. Jim Turrell and Patty Turrell, two individuals who are the personification of servanthood. They are two of my most trusted guardian angels. My spiritual family at O.C. Spiritual Center, Center for Spiritual Living Huntington Beach, and Center for Spiritual Living Capistrano Valley. This includes everyone I encountered (living or dead) since I began my journey with the Science of Mind philosophy in 2012, even those individuals I didn't have the pleasure of getting to know in depth.

Rev. Janet Moore and Rev. Carla Schiratis, are two leaders whose dedication to their role as ministers inspires me. We've had incredible moments together, filled with laughter and lots of love. I am grateful.

All the Licensed Prayer Practitioners I worked with individually or collectively with a special shout-out to those practitioners at O.C. Spiritual Center: Anne Perrah, Afrah Salahuddin, Bob Estrada, Ginni Gordon, J.R. Mendivil, Kyle Moore, Marion Whitson, Nancy Jo Clark, Natasha Meskal, and Richard Jarvis. And I include posthumously, Dan Castle and Syndi Jones.

Members of the monthly support group, Community First, at O.C. Spiritual Center: Beverly & Jerry Bigelow,

188

A Love Letter to Thomas

Karen Lindsay, Kathy Greco, Jim Ringle, and David Watkins.

Two friends who I have been the closest to over the years, Teri (Blair) Broughton, and Julie (Armenta) Smith. These ladies have demonstrated what true friendship means. I appreciate you ladies and am grateful to be on this journey with you.

Jim Cramer, founder of Spirit Tours. You and your team, including children Gitana and Tim, provided incredible opportunities for me to explore spirituality during our group trips to Bali, Ireland, and Bhutan. These experiences opened my heart up to other cultures, belief systems, and ways of living. Travel is the only thing that makes us richer, right? You proved that time and time again through your servant leadership, for which I am eternally grateful. Namaste.

Four individuals whose love for each other at the perfect, right time allowed Thomas and me to be birthed into this existence: Michele (LeDrogoff) Chauvel, Bernard Chauvel, Phylis (Fulton, Uhler) Coates, and Raymond Uhler. Our ancestors are still cheering us on!

Dear friends and neighbors who came to my aid in the early days and months of my new normal, bringing food, prayer, resources, gifts, and their presence to sooth my soul: Kathleen Carroll, Lisa Sutton, Dave Holman, Lori & Paul Curtis, Maile Busby, Brian Lindley, Phyllis Speek, Chuck & Gayle Jensen (who opened up their home to my relative from France), Shirley & Norm Pruitt, Michelle & Scott Trippanera, Mona Rosenberg, Deborah Khoshaba-Maddi & Sal Maddi, Virginia & Bruce Holler, Steve Blackwell.

Anyone and everyone who reached out to me via

social media. Yes, this a blanket statement which I am allowed to make, right? I'm grateful to live in an age where we can connect with each other in an instant.

Special thanks to Beatrice Foster for counseling me on writing, giving me her listening ear, and pushing me in ways only I know internally. Our conversations opened new perspectives for me, allowing the creative source to flow with a stronger sense of purpose. Your strength is to be revered.

All helpers, first responders (Scott Phillips - EMT, Logan Rodriguez – EMT, Eric Hintze – AEMT, and Jonathan Jahp – AEMT/Driver), and health care workers who were put to task on February 6, 2020. The team at University of Health Utah in Salt Lake City. Witnesses to the accident (according to the Park City police report): Philip Bannes, Deirdre Masterton, Matt Wollschleger, Terry & Susan Hlavinka, Jeremy Musser, and Alex Rousselot.

Colin King, Melissa Tabish and the entire team at Dewsnup King Olsen Woral Havas Mortensen. The team at Summit County District Attorney's Office, specifically Trish Cassell.

Self-care practices play a critical role in my overall health. They kicked into high gear after Thomas' death and during the writing of this book. A significant part of these practices involve forgiveness, fully directing this aspect to those involved in Thomas' death. That said, I publicly declare that I forgive 'Watson.' May he have the courage to move forward from this circumstance, with peace and with love.

Special thanks to my Personal Care Team: Dr. Daisy Tint at Memorial Care (my primary care physician of over

20 years who is now retired), Dr. Darlene Lara of Santé Pilates Studio in Corona del Mar, Lanae Dahl (masseuse extraordinaire), Cristal and Holly at Blü Nail Bar in Fashion Island, Jennifer Brown, R.N. & Danielle Miller R.N. at Natural Illumination in Newport Beach, coaches at WORK Training Studio in Irvine, yoga instructors at CorePower, Reiki Master Kathy Brook-Wong (OnWingsOfJoy.com) and Taba at TY Alexander Salon in Newport Beach. (I like to joke that Taba is the only man outside of family members with whom I have had the longest relationship.)

Frank Coon & staff at Independent Funeral Service in Salt Lake City, Utah. Devan Bobo, Victim Advocate Coordinator, Park City Police Department. Asay Engineering and Jewkes Biomechanics. Judge Mrazik whom I trusted implicitly to use his judgement when overseeing the criminal case.

All those who were fortunate enough to be in the presence of Thomas Chauvel during his 43 years of life, on land or sea. A special nod to Laurent Vrignaud and his staff at Moulin. You gave Thomas a French family here in the U.S. which allowed him to feel more comfortable being an immigrant. Merci beaucoup (French for thank you) to Sam Geffroy, owner of Roquette in Costa Mesa. The stories you tell about Thomas warm my heart. It's such a treat to have you in Orange County, preparing traditional dishes from Brittany that bring back lovely memories.

My editors, Dr. Anne Perrah & John Lunsford. You two ran the gauntlet for me in ways I cannot describe. Your patience, guidance, and loving support provided me with the motivation to continue moving through the writing process despite forces that were pulling me away from it. Your compliments on my writing ability (and future promise) blew me away, high praise coming from well-established writers and educators.

Last, but not least, members of the Anti Social-Distancing Club – Janet Moore, Steve Williams, Afrah Salahuddin, and Hugh Foster. The five of us gathered at my home which Hugh dubbed the "speakevesy" one night a week, every week, for six months straight, starting in late March 2020 going through September 2020. Those experiences provided a safety net for all of us, with multiple opportunities to laugh, dance, and play games. Each week had a different theme and costume suggestion. We connected in fun and love which led to greater revelations about ourselves. Those moments are a treasure trove of delights, forever engraved on my heart. Thank you.

Science of Mind – What We Believe

We believe in God, the Living Spirit Almighty; one, indestructible, absolute, and self-existent Cause. This One manifests Itself in and through all creation but is not absorbed by Its creation. The manifest universe is the body of God; it is the logical and necessary outcome of the infinite self-knowingness of God.

We believe in the individualization of the Spirit in us, and that all people are individualizations of the One Spirit.

We believe in the eternality, the immortality, and the continuity of the individual soul, forever and ever expanding.

We believe that heaven is within us, and that we experience it to the degree that we become conscious of it.

We believe the ultimate goal of life to be a complete freedom from all discord of every nature, and that this goal is sure to be attained by all.

We believe in the unity of all life, and that the highest God and the innermost God is one God. We believe that God is personal to all who feel this indwelling presence.

We believe in the direct revelation of truth through our intuitive and spiritual nature, and that anyone may become a revealer of truth who lives in close contact with the indwelling God.

Eve Chauvel

We believe that the Universal Spirit, which is God, operated through a Universal Mind, which is the Law of God, and that we are surrounded by this Creative Mind which receives the direct impress of our thought and acts upon it.

We believe in the healing of the sick and control of condition through the power of this Mind.

We believe in the eternal Goodness, the eternal Loving-kindness and the eternal Givingness of Life to All.

We believe in our own soul, our own spirit and our own destiny; for we understand that the life of all is God.

A Love Letter to Thomas

Resources

To make a donation in the memory of Thomas Chauvel:

Arbor Day Foundation – arborday.org/ 1-888-448-7337

or

Orange Coast College Foundation
Thomas Chauvel Memorial Fund
Culinary Arts Program
https://orangecoastcollege.edu/about/foundation/giving-to-occ.html
1-714-432-5126

or

Check payable to *Orange Coast College, Foundation* with Thomas Chauvel Memorial Fund in the memo mailed to:
Orange Coast College, Foundation
2701 Fairview Road
Costa Mesa, CA 92626

Chapman, Gary. *The Secret to Love that Lasts.* Chicago:Northfield Publishing, 2014.

Chodron, Pema. *When Things Fall Apart.* Boulder: Shambhala, 1996.

Cousineau, Phil. *Soul Moments: Marvelous Stories of Synchronicity — Meaningful Coincidences from a Seemingly Random World.* Berkeley: Conari Press, 1997.

de Saint-Exupéry, Antoine. *The Little Prince.* Orlando: Harcourt Inc., 1943, 2000.

Didion, Joan. *The Year of Magical Thinking.* New York: Knopf Doubleday Publishing, 2007.

Hanh, Thich Nhat. *Fear: Essential Wisdom for Getting Through the Storm.* New York: HarperCollins, 2014.

Hickman, Martha. *Healing After Loss.* New York: HarperCollins, 1994, 2002.

Holmes, Ernest. *Living the Science of Mind.* Camarillo: DeVorss & Company, 1984.

Holmes, Ernest. *How to Use The Science of Mind: Principle in Practice.* Golden: Science of Mind Publishing, 2009.

Holmes, Ernest. *This Thing Called You.* London: Penguin Group USA, 1948, 2004.

Holmes, Ernest. *The Science of Mind: A Philosophy, A Faith, A Way of Life.* New York: Penguin Random House, 1938, 2012.

Jones, Dennis Merritt. *How to Speak Science of Mind A Seeker's Guide to the Basic Concepts and Terms That Define this Practical Spiritual Lifestyle.* Camarillo: DeVorss & Company, 2010.

Jones, Dennis Merritt. *The Art of Uncertainty: How to Live in the Mystery of Life and Love It.* New York: Penguin Group, 2011.

Kessler, David. *Finding Meaning: The Sixth Stage of Grief.* London: Penguin Random House UK, 2019.

Kübler-Ross, Elisabeth and David Kessler. *On Grief and Grieving: Finding the Meaning of Grief Through the Five Stages of Loss.* New York: Scribner, 2014.

Lowe, Al and Martha Ann Stewart. *Concordance to The Science of Mind.* Golden: Science of Mind Publishing, 1974.

McInerny, Nora. *The Hot Young Widows Club: Lessons on Survival from the Front Lines of Grief.* New York: Simon and Schuster, 2019.

Mellonie, Bryan and Robert Ingpen. *Lifetimes: The beautiful way to explain death to children.* Sydney: Bantam Books, 1983.

Moore, Thomas. *Dark Nights of the Soul: A Guide to Finding Your Way Through Life's Ordeals.* New York: Penguin Random House, 2004.

Peale, Norman Vincent. *The Power of Positive Thinking.* Parsippany: Simon & Schuster, 2003.

Perrah, Anne. *Taken to Heart: Parenting Our Children and Re-Parenting Ourselves Through the Healing Power of Story.* Cypress: NuFreedom Press, 2013.

Perry, Bruce D. and Oprah Winfrey. *What Happened to You? Conversations on Trauma, Resilience, and Healing.* New York: Flatiron Books, 2021.

Rankin, Eric Steven. *As Above, So Below: The Quantum Teachings of Jesus.* Las Vegas: Cedarwoods, 2023.

Ruiz, Don Miguel. *The Four Agreements.* San Rafael: Amber-Allen Publishing, 1997.

Science of Mind Magazine. Golden: Science of Mind Publishing (https://scienceofmind.com/)

Smith, Deanna Allcorn. *A Year On The Journey: Your companion in co-creating a truly useful and fulfilling relationship with God.* Bloomington: Hay House, 2022.

The Hardiness Institute (www.hardinessinstitute.com)

Tolle, Eckhart. *The Power of Now.* Novato: New World Library, 1999.

Turrell, Jim. *How To Complete A Relationship.* Costa Mesa: CSL Publishers, 2013.

Turrell, Jim. *When It's Time to Leave.* Costa Mesa: HeartTalk Publishing, 2015.

Williams, Paul and Tracey Jackson,. *Gratitude & Trust.* New York: Penguin Press, 2014.